THE BEST OF CIVILIZATION

An Anthology from the *Questions of Civilization*
Program at Claremont McKenna College

Robert J. Valenza, Editor

PORTLAND • OREGON
INKWATERPRESS.COM

TABLE OF CONTENTS

PREFACE

THE *QUESTIONS OF CIVILIZATION* Program at Claremont McKenna College began its trial run during the fall semester of 1996. There were only four sections then, taught by Profs. Jay Martin, James Nichols, John Poynter and me. The following year it was accepted by our full faculty as a freshman general education requirement, with Prof. Martin as the inaugural program director. I became its director in 2000 and still serve as such at the time of this writing; much more to the point, I have had the privilege of teaching in this program every year since its inception.

This program is something of a Great Books course, a freshman seminar, and a general introduction to academic discourse. Whatever its exact nature, it stands out in our curriculum as nondisciplinary, predisciplinary, transdisciplinary—take your pick. We designed the course to address great issues, without any disciplinary bias, much as one might look at the earth from space and not see its artificial division into appropriately labeled nations. We also wanted to encourage a great deal of flexibility in how it was taught, and so only about half of the course readings are common to all sections; the rest are at the particular instructor's discretion. Above all, it was the nearly universal will of the faculty that this course should be in no way *doctrinaire*. That may sound a simple enough goal—if somewhat unusual for college professors accustomed to holding forth nonstop in their respective areas of expertise—but, nonetheless, I want to say a little more about it in order to convey something essential about the course.

No one would call a professor of astronomy doctrinaire for teaching that the planets move, to a fine approximation, in elliptical orbits around the sun. Why not? Evidently because the planets really do move in this way. Stating the facts of the world, as mathematics and science always intend, is just stating the truth. Yet when we choose to talk instead of the meaning of being human, goodness, religion, civic obligations, art, and knowledge of the world in general, we rapidly move away from the hard boundaries that constrain the terms and truth values attached to scientific propositions. We move, rather, into a world of objects and standards of truth that are soft, fuzzy, and even nebulous. In this hazy world, being doctrinaire *does* mean something: it means establishing, in advance, terms, truths and standards that are beyond questioning; it means a pretense at stronger truth values than can be objectively justified; it means that the student submits to the authority of the professional. All of that is just what we wanted to avoid.

Thus *Questions of Civilization* came into being as a course devoted to enormous questions with no pretense to final answers—and certainly not to answers served up in lectures to be passively transcribed by students into the ephemera of their notebooks. It became a course that gave inquiry priority over conclusion and encouraged students to speak in loud, passionate, but always *informed* voices. It became a place where students might say large risky things about big issues and set aside the tinny voice and timid attitude that too often characterize the safe modes of discourse within a narrow disciplinary perspective. With this, again by intention, came a blurring of the line between matters of academic detachment and matters of life. Indeed, one of our main points has been that a liberal arts education—in fact, any education worth having—must have something to say directly about the most significant choices we make in our everyday lives, and about our way of seeing and being in the world.

So what are these enormous questions, the questions that govern the constitution of societies and the everyday lives of their constituents? Here they are—each, in a sense, subsidiary to the first:

What does it mean to be human?
What is a good person?
What is the role of the individual in society?
What is the nature of knowledge and science?
What is the nature of religion and religious experience?
What is the nature of art and aesthetic experience?
What is the nature of human diversity?

This last question is not mere political correctness: it is the question, as old as the Cro-Magnon and the Neanderthals, of what we do when we encounter The Other.

So, given the freedom and responsibility to begin to develop an informed personal philosophy, how does a highly select and talented group of ambitious, overachieving freshmen respond? That is exactly what this anthology is about.

The essays herein give voice to the developing thoughts of our students. They are chosen from over a span of nearly a decade, from fall of 1998 to spring of this year. The range of topics is vast, and the treatments range from the austerely abstract to the intimately personal. Always the opinions expressed—for right or for wrong, for better or for worse—are those of the writers, not of the program or the institution. One may find lacunae in the knowledge base, errors or quirks in the interpretation of famous works, positions that anticipate or echo those of prominent scholars left unmentioned because they were simply still unknown to the young writer, occasional intemperate categoricals, etc. But these are not research papers, and to hint at something of the penultimate essay in this collection, they are the early residue of works of art in progress.[1] Many of these papers are not the product of the orderly development of a rigid outline, but of a lyrical, organic process that reflects the unpredictable intellectual and emotional growth of its author. If this costs something in academic elegance—and I'm not sure it does—it buys a degree of vividness, intensity and authenticity that would be difficult to match.

I must add one observation that I could not have made without the experience of having assembled this collection. Among the commonly read texts in this course, two stand out as having made an indelible impression, and both are works of literature. My guess—and I will not stoop to counting—is that the two most referenced works here are *The Death of Ivan Ilych* by Leo Tolstoy and Jane Austen's *Sense and Sensibility*. I mention this because Ivan from the former work and the sisters Elinor and Marianne from the latter seem to have taught these students more about ethics, epistemology and human nature than anything from giants such as Plato, Aristotle and Freud. Parents and teachers, take note.

Finally, let me acknowledge the support of my colleagues Elenor Taylor and Elizabeth Morgan whose students are also well represented in this enterprise. I thank, too, my wife Brenda, who volunteered to do an astute and much-needed round of editing and proofreading with a fresh pair of eyes—in fact, beautiful brown ones. Her work significantly raised the quality of the final product.

---

[1] To preserve a sense of informality and to enhance the flow for the reader, I have deleted most of the full academic citations from these essays. A brief bibliography appears at the end of the collection, and this will resolve most questions of reference. For instance, a simple reference to Freud will be to *Civilization and Its Discontents* and, specifically, to the particular edition noted.

The final boulder has been shouldered aside. We feel a freshet of cool, wet air from the suddenly revealed access to an underground cavern of dimensions we only begin to surmise. After wriggling through the opening, we make our way across the undefined space to a splintered wooden chest bound by black bands of iron. Now, in the expectant silence, the lid is creakily raised. There, within its musty, dim confines, lie the gems: a vast, sparkling variety of shapes, facets, transparencies, opacities, hues, iridescences and luminosities. We behold the most precious objects of the universe: living minds.

Robert Valenza
Alta Loma, California
Summer, 2007

The Importance of Tradition

Sophia Hall

ALTHOUGH MANY PEOPLE IN WESTERN society may not agree with *The Analects of Confucius*, I believe that Confucius has eloquently and succinctly defined the importance of family and tradition in society. Today, more and more people in the western world, especially in the United States, define their lives by individualism and reject tradition because they believe it restricts and confines their freedoms. Others live in societies where they are completely bound to tradition. Neither extreme of these lifestyles is a healthy or successful way to live. Rather, I believe it is important to preserve the sense of tradition and culture while exploring one's sense of individualism. When referring to tradition, I do not mean a severe, rigid, traditional society, but a balanced, tolerant society founded upon tradition. I believe that balancing tradition and filial piety with self-definition and self-expression is the key to living the healthiest life possible.

Although many tend to look at only the disadvantages of tradition, there are numerous benefits of living in a traditional society. Tradition brings stability to society by establishing a regulation of how humans interact with each other. If everyone of us did what we wanted, when we wanted, and without concern for others, it would be a very disorderly and dangerous world to live in. With tradition also comes a sense of identity and belonging. For children, community and tradition are necessary because they provide a sense of belonging. When people grow older, this sense of community in fact *helps* individuals self-actualize and define themselves in relation to their community. This notion is contrary to what some might believe because some think that tradition hinders self-expression when it actually provides a foundation for individualism by instilling values and culture. Although one is a member in a group, one can define oneself and be an individual within the group. Tradition does not take that sense of self-identity or individualism away, but rather complements and strengthens it. The establishment of values, for example, that comes with tradition sets up the foundation for one's moral and spiritual life. This value system serves as guidance for adults as well as children, especially when there are difficulties encountered in life. Finally, through tradition, one is taught a sense of decency, common sense and especially respect toward family, but also toward others. Respect is the fundamental underlying concept behind tradition and is needed for a well-functioning and cohesive community.

Finding the balance between tradition and individualism is crucial to living the best life possible. According to Confucius, "Filial piety and fraternal duty—surely they are the roots of humaneness." (Book 1, #2) I agree with this statement and the overall concept of duty towards family. The emphasis of Confucius on love and respect for family is something that I believe should be emphasized in today's world. However, I do not believe that tradition and fraternal duty should be excessive to a point where a society becomes restricting, oppressive and intolerant. If one is chained strictly to tradition, then one does not have much flexibility to make individual choices. I feel that one should not be bound to tradition to the extent that Confucius instructs because I believe individualism can exist in harmony with the traditional aspect of a society. In my opinion, Confucianism does not leave room for individuality. In contrast, those who entirely reject traditionalism argue one cannot be happy and self-actualize when living in a traditional society. I believe, however, that they have not experienced or been exposed to a functional traditional society—one where you can self-actualize while still respecting others and valuing the ways of one's parents and ancestors. I lived in a country characterized by tradition and culture, yet it was a society that allowed, nonetheless, for progress, tolerance of self-definition, and the expression of individuality.

Morocco, a country defined by tradition and culture, was not always a place of tolerance. In the past, because of tradition, it was an illiterate society that was not able to deal with the onslaught of the European world. Yet it has uniquely adapted because tradition is maintained while progress and self-definition are encouraged. A compelling example of this is marriage. Arranged marriages have existed in Moroccan society for many years because girls did not leave their homes often to interact with many persons other than family. Therefore, the fathers had to look for a companion who they thought would support their daughter. There has since been a change: girls are highly educated and work outside the home, allowing them to meet people they could possibly marry. My grandmother's marriage was arranged for she did not go to school; my mom, however, did not have an arranged marriage. In fact, she chose to marry a foreigner, which was even more daring and uncommon. Yet her father still consented to the union. People can choose their companion, but tradition comes into play when asking the consent of family. There is a special ceremony where the man has to formally ask the bride's father's consent at the family house. The man brings presents and offerings for the bride. There used to be a dowry paid to the family of the bride, which would be dictated by the father of the bride. Today, the groom decides the amount of money to give the bride to pay for things for the wedding. However, the groom still has to proceed with the formal ceremony with all the traditional aspects entailed. It is out of respect that one does this; it does not mean that one is oppressed by elders or family to act a certain way. This is an example of the adaptation of tradition, where tradition and culture are preserved while allowing for free-willed individual choices. When I get married, whether to a Moroccan or foreigner, my future husband will still have to ask for my father's consent in the same traditional way that has been done for centuries, simply out of respect.

As exemplified by Moroccan society and tradition, there can be an attainable middle ground between an oppressively traditional and dangerously individualist society. I believe the healthiest society to live in is a traditional one that adapts to changing circumstances in today's world. Tradition is important in a society because it teaches respect for family, elders, and mentors who are valued for their past experiences in life. Younger generations can benefit from this knowledge. Finally, not only does tradition encourage respect for loved ones, it also encourages respect for traditions of others. I value the traditions and culture of Morocco and believe tradition should be a fundamental part of everyone's life.

RATIONALITY AND ROMANCE

Eric Ren

INDIVIDUALS IN CIVILIZATION EXHIBIT a need to express themselves, to define their own existence and to experience the fullness of life. This is part of human nature. But someone who characterizes this desire to the extreme would be viewed by society as both unorthodox and irrational. The practical realist may see the romantic idealist as too dramatic and detached from the real world. In contrast, the romantic may not want to live a life that is predictable and mechanical, as often associated with an attitude of rationality and social responsibility. In the personal sense, both these outlooks on life apply well in certain cases, and in the societal sense, both these qualities hold great value. This leads me to the conclusion that balance is key to personal or societal success.

The contrast between rationality and emotion is embodied in Elinor and Marianne, the two main characters in Jane Austen's *Sense and Sensibility*.

Elinor represents sense, reason, and social responsibility. If her character were placed in a completely dark room, she would most likely feel around carefully and deliberately, taking in what she can from her senses, objectifying it, verifying her conclusions, and continue to repeat the process as she moved across the room. In general, it is advantageous to have Elinor's traits when, figuratively speaking, it would be disastrous to fall in the dark. When dealing with personal finance, for example, one hasty decision or one wrong investment could have enormous costs. Buying a house, choosing a career path, or even choosing whom to marry are all decisions that require a lot of reasoning and judgment. It would seem that in long-term plans or in keeping long-term relationships, having the wisdom of Elinor would be very beneficial.

However, these are all personal reasons why someone might choose to behave like Elinor. On a deeper level, Elinor's approach to life, interpreting things objectively and for what they are, has great value in a broader sense as well. Elinor's epistemic stance is based on the correspondence theory of truth; it is objective, it corresponds to the facts, and it is sharable. One of the ultimate values of truth is that it binds humanity together, and having certain shared truths or world views is crucial to the success of a civilization. Having a shared subjectivity among people not only increases the sense of community, which benefits individuals in their search for love and meaning, but also forms the basis for human interaction. If people made everything they sensed personal and incorporated it into their own private truths, there would be nothing that connects one person to another, no common ground among humans. The benefit of collective truth is, perhaps, part of why religion has helped the rise of many civilizations, and is seen by some rulers as something useful.

Because of the importance of rational thought in personal decision-making and the value of having truths that are shared by all, having Elinor's "sense" in a society and as an individual is essential. But is it enough? As we have seen in many works like Socrates' *Antigone* and Shakespeare's *King Lear*, truth does not always lead to happiness. Furthermore, it is very hard to imagine a society with individuals content in living very ordered, mechanical lives and following very predictable paths guided by tradition and social responsibility. People want to choose, to create, to reach a certain level of self-definition, and to have rich personal experiences. Elinor's "sense" seems hardly to satisfy these desires, and the missing key may lie in the other principal character from *Sense and Sensibility*.

Marianne, the younger of the two sisters, symbolizes "sensibility," which represents emotion, passion, and spontaneity. Because she senses, interprets by private standards, and then acts without much verification, she would not be as careful in the hypothetical dark room as Elinor. However, one can argue that Marianne would be likely to have more fun than Elinor in navigating through the room, or at least have a "richer" experience. Because Marianne dramatizes events, she may have a slightly distorted view on the objective nature of the world. Nevertheless, sometimes the personal gain from experiencing the world like this may be worth the risks or costs involved. For example, many people would choose a Marianne approach when forming new relationships. To feel like you are choosing your friends and making the most out of the uncertainty and spontaneity of the population far outweighs the potential consequences of making a wrong impression or a bad judgment. Passion and spontaneity also have vital roles in society as a whole. Many inventions, scientific breakthroughs, and great pieces of art are brought about by devoted individuals who are able to harness spur-of-the-moment forces, even if they are nurtured and made possible by order and discipline. In essence, it is important to have a certain degree of chaos within order, and both are central to the prosperity of civilization.

It makes sense to say that in personal development, a balance between Elinor's character and Marianne's character is ideal, while still maintaining the flexibility to move towards one side of the spectrum or another according to the situation. Odysseus in Homer's *Odyssey* characterizes this balance very well, taking calculated risks while still being able to control his emotions. In a broader sense, society also needs a balance of reason, rationality and structure versus passion, emotion, and spontaneity. The Enlightenment period in the 18th Century emphasized rationality and "sense" in its systems of knowledge, ethics, and philosophy, while the Romanticism that followed rejected order and harmony for the imaginative, emotional and subjective—the "sensibility" side of the balance. If the Aristotelian mean between those extremes is indeed optimal, I cannot help but wonder if we have yet reached that balance today.

REFLECTIONS IN A PHOTOGRAPH

Tracey Aragon

ART IS THE COMMUNICATION of emotions. Many enjoy a piece of art because they can relate it to their experiences. However, sometimes the emotions that the spectators gather from art may not be what the artist intended. For example, the photographer Gloria Chang stimulated my emotions with her untitled photograph without meaning to do so. She simply believed that the red would look wonderful on black and white. Although she did not intend to evoke an emotion, she captivated a part of my life and faith.

The photograph shows that there is something more than just living. There is passion, love for others, and love for the things we wish to achieve. The black and white represents society's standards, but the color red demonstrates our passion to pursue our faith and the meaning of life. One should not remain caged up like the bird in the picture; one should instead fly to achieve ones goals.

The young woman in the photograph has not yet started to live her own life. She has lived in society's cage which is covered by a piece of cloth with red flowers; the cloth of others' desires. The suppressors who blind us in order to pursue *their* visions, dreams, and goals have shoved us into a cage where we are controlled by their authority for their own benefit. For instance, I was raised in a Catholic community which taught me that there is no other truth but God. I have been trained to believe that we should only venerate God and that those who did not were evil. Moreover, like the young woman in the photograph, I have begun to search for my own suppositions.

The young woman in the photograph has begun to set her own standards. Her red high heels will lead her into a world where she can pursue her desires. The heels represent her strength to stand up to the world. I have just found the world where I can decide what I want for myself without having others tell me what I should believe. I am beginning to write the lyrics of my own song. I am slowly coming out of the cage in order to put together my beliefs to express myself, to love, and to achieve my goals freely.

I have begun to question the religious faith that I was taught and have realized that I disagree with a couple of Catholic beliefs. I wish that the principles of my religion were sometimes different. I believe in only one God, but there are others who perform good deeds and do not believe in my God. A fundamental belief of my religion is that even those who are good people but do not believe in God will go to hell. This is almost impossible for me to accept. Those who perform benevolent acts deserve a piece of heaven whether they have a belief in God or not. They are helping God by helping others, since God is in each of us. Although I have established some beliefs of my own, there is more to question and to consider before I reach my final conclusions about religion. There is more to learn in order to fight the battles against those who impose their will.

I am the young woman in the photograph who has been trying to live. I have been fighting through the hardship of the standards of society to find myself. Life is not about what others want me to do, yet it is about my own desires. I must show the world that I am not confined by others' regimes in forming my core beliefs and values. I must show the world that I can think for myself. Thinking for oneself makes the world a beautiful, colorful, and interesting piece of art.

Photograph by Gloria Chang. Reprinted with permission.

SAVAGES AND SONGBIRDS

Daniel O'Toole

MORE THAN ANYTHING ELSE, the texts in *Civilization* challenged my understanding of human nature. Knowing human nature helps us determine how individuals ought to act and how society ought to treat them. It shapes the values on which civilizations are founded and the purposes for which men lead their lives. The fundamental question I found myself contemplating during the course is whether man is depraved or innocent—savage or songbird.

The challenge of human nature forms the central contradiction in my beliefs. Religiously and philosophically, I am an absolutist. I believe man is made in the image of God and aspires to serve Him on earth. Moral action defends and respects the dignity of all men and ensures their freedom. This side of me rests faith in a Natural Law, and it can call for idealism, optimism, and at times revolution in order to enhance the human condition. Man has freewill and thus must own responsibility for his actions. Compassion should be his prime motivation as he strives to live a moral, purposeful life. In an ideal world, everyone would resemble Atticus Finch from *To Kill a Mockingbird*.

Politically, however, I am a relativist and a realist. My observations of mankind's history only make me pessimistic. Chaos and irrationality dominate over man's civil side. Failure to recognize these Machiavellian and Hobbesian tendencies in men and to respond aggressively leaves one vulnerable to violence and oppression from his fellow humans. Self-interest determines man's actions and frequently leads him to brutal aggression against others. Those values that he does espouse, he has merely internalized from his society. In this worldview, he should be judged in the context of his social circumstance rather than by universal principles. I also believe security and social order are the first orders of government. Likewise, tradition and culture demand respect, and rebels like Antigone and Alden Pyle in Graham Greene's *The Quiet American* cause more suffering than they prevent.

Most of the texts seemed to support the pessimistic view of human nature. Euripides' *Medea* most clearly shows a society built on reason and goodwill failing to understand and cope with the savage, Medea. Hot emotions—jealousy, passion, and vengeance—drive Medea. The Greek world of Jason shields itself from foreigners and blinds itself to the frontiers of anarchy seeping into its borders. There is little doubt throughout the play that Jason also has self-interested motives. He desires the crown and a younger wife. However, Jason fails to recognize the more primitive, animalistic motives at play. He invents elaborate rationalizations for his switching partners that include the benefit of his family. Medea, of course, sees straight through his careful, civilized rationalizing. She condemns Jason, saying that "a wicked man who is most eloquent seems most wicked of all."

Jason and the people of Corinth fail to prevent Medea's atrocities because they fail to understand her. Jason writes off Medea's emotions as "ungoverned rage." Creon fatally gives Medea an extra day to leave, allowing her to carry out her murders. Her neighbors and the chorus realize her plans, but even they fail to stop her. These people of reason cannot comprehend the irrational. Thus, Medea unleashes ruthless tragedy with ease, killing both king and princess before murdering her own children to avenge Jason.

Although Jason's coldness bears part of the guilt for his children's deaths, what interests me most is that Jason and the people of Corinth fail to stop Medea. Fear and civility paralyze them. A world beyond reason mystifies them, and most importantly, they fail to recognize man's dark heart. Even Jason's dark desires and naked ambitions have a hand in the murder of his children. Had Creon properly understood the extent of Medea's evil, he could have banished her immediately. The citizens, knowing where her plans were going, could have stood up and stopped Medea.

For practical political philosophy, one must accept that self-interest at best and evil at worst shape the human heart. Recent history falls in line with this conclusion. America botched its effort in Iraq by underestimating the violence of Sunnis displaced from power and the hatred of Jihadists trying to foil the U.S. Faith in reason—that all Iraqis would embrace freedom— and a timid fear of casualties have prevented the U.S. from both providing enough troops and supporting a long-term strategy for victory. Many watched with horror as law and order broke down in the wealthiest nation in the world after Hurricane Katrina. Absent governing authority, selfish desires and Hobbesian anarchy took over. Likewise, enlightened Europe seems shrouded from reality and bears an eerie resemblance to the noble Greek city-states. Aloof in what some call a postmodern paradise, Europeans refuse to support a substantial defense budget and military ventures abroad in an increasingly hostile world. At home, Europe fails to assimilate Muslim immigrants, and, instead, these outsiders remain the Medeas of self-segregated cities. In this light, the riots that erupted in the French suburbs seem hardly surprising.

One must conclude that violence is a natural propensity for men. If men act out of selfish desires, then one must be ready to do violence to protect his own personhood against the selfish desires of others. Accepting this proposition, that one can harm another to defend himself, seems to acknowledge a shade of moral relativism. It denies a categorical restraint on violence against another human being. Even self-defense challenges the freewill and human dignity of the enemy. But to not act this way is silly. A human being with no selfish interests does not exist. The wisest men recognize the evil that exists in all people and do not limit the tools they have to deal with such evil.

The most frightening example of the failure to comprehend evil was depicted in the movie *Der Untergang*. Hitler's insane cruelty and the zealotry of his closest followers are not the most damning things shown in the film. Rather, the guilt of the secretary as an old woman at the end is the most piercing part of the movie. Common citizens had a role in electing and supporting Hitler. His hate made him appealing, and he tapped into the everyday frustrations of Germans. The woman at the end recognizes her role in the Holocaust. Just as she failed to prevent it, the West failed to halt the Holocaust and Hitler's expansion across Europe. Appeasement, the natural folly of those more accustomed to the rational than the irrational, let Nazism rise to power in Europe. Few wanted to hear the voices demanding early action against Hitler's aggression. This missed opportunity made the devastating Second World War inevitable.

Hitler was a savage; but more importantly, he was a revolutionary. Revolutionaries seek to overturn social institutions in the name of justice and progress. Revolutionary ideologies, from communism to modern Islamic fascism, and movements that seek to overturn the status quo have historically spurred the bloodiest of wars. Even shifts in power balances throw societies into chaos. For this reason, I find revolutionaries poisonous. They carry out the tragedy of human history. Idealists such as Greene's Pyle tear people from the life they know. In the process they ignore the difficulty of change and the complexities of social reality. For this reason, Pyle believes aiding General Thé, a merciless terrorist, will actually help the people of Vietnam. Indeed all friends of dramatic social change, including the communists and the imperialists, prove horribly inept and murderous.

The best counter to a savage and dangerous world is a solid social order. *The Analects of Confucius* points out that "culture is just as important as the stuff one is made of." Respect for tradition and institutions lays the foundation for stability and security. Moral systems, government, religion, and families help define the individual's role in his society. They preserve harmony and deter destructive behavior. Individuals challenging the social order demand fierce punishment. The suitors in Homer's *Odyssey* do not respect the gods or Odysseus' rule of Ithaca. They defame his marriage and challenge all authority. For this reason, Odysseus responds to their savage behavior with equally savage violence—he slaughters them without remorse. Similarly, in Aristophanes' *The Clouds*, Strepsiades burns down Socrates' thinkery in order to protect social harmony over the perceived threat to religion, family, and justice.

But how much do I trust social order? I remember shouting in class that if the system is rotten, it has to go. At some point, the individual must question whether security justifies oppression. This is where my view of man as a songbird takes hold. The wretched cruelty in the novels *Beloved* and *To Kill a Mockingbird* stirs the heart. Adopting a relativist view can merely shrug off racism as a mere cultural construct. In such a view, the actions of the schoolteacher character from *Beloved*, judged in context of his social circumstance, cannot be condemned. Such cold moral indifference, however, also runs counter to human nature.

People feel compassion every day for others' suffering. Freud might argue this tendency merely reflects our morals internalized from society--our superego. I find this claim an incomplete explanation of man's sense of morality. Compassion can be seen across cultures. Our feeling of justice hardly stems from a personal insecurity. I believe people can act out of genuine empathy. Furthermore, it seems that once one recognizes his conscience as simply the voice of civilization, he can easily act beyond its parameters. However, people constantly constrain themselves for the good of others even when they reject social values and see no benefit to their self-interest. The same intuition that tells us cruelty on another is immoral also tells us that self-interest is not the whole sum of human characteristics.

Universal human dignity is self-evident. Man may be born a flexible and bendable species, and he may have a natural inclination towards evil, but I believe there must be some good— a songbird—inside. From a Christian view, he can transcend his fallen nature. Indeed, I cannot avoid Antigone's yearning for compassion, freedom, and humanity in the face of rigid law. Nor can I ignore Atticus' call for justice and love against a rotten social order. Of course it was absurd for the jury to vote for Tom Robison's guilt simply to preserve the social harmony in *To Kill a Mockingbird*. I even find myself siding with Socrates. A being as thoughtful as man cannot avoid seeking the truth. He may upset people, challenge their values, and make them insecure, but the truth has worth that outweighs the pain it causes.

So how can one hold these contradicting notions of human nature? How can I be pragmatic and compassionate, realistic and optimistic, conservative and revolutionary? Maybe I can never reconcile these contradictions. Maybe the Atticus Finches of the world will always leave their children vulnerable to the many Bob Ewells. But I like to think that this challenge is simply man's burden: to understand the cynical, but to still seek the good. It means compromise. It means using force at times in order to preserve a greater good. When I think of the atrocities in *Medea*, *Der Untergang*, and *The Quiet American*, I do not merely think of the failure of civilization to protect itself. I feel compassion for the innocent dead. Yes, there is a songbird in every man, just as every man can be a savage. The struggle to do right in a world of perpetual injustice is the fundamental challenge of mankind.

A Matter of Conscience, a Matter of History: The Role of the Individual in Society

Nandini Majumdar

IT IS EVERY INDIVIDUAL'S responsibility, in a democratic society, to constantly question and to educate herself about the workings of that society of which she is a part. Then, if she does not agree with the 'laws' of that society—the premises upon which that society works—it is her responsibility to act upon her belief. There are many types of action, and I believe non-violent action to be the best.

The definition of responsibility I have put forth works at several levels. History tells us that the spirit of questioning and the desire for change is an unusual one. Over time, human communities have not been characterized by a public restlessness for reform; it is individuals who have been. These individuals, from Socrates to Martin Luther King, stand out as the single initiators of new thought and action, as the 'leaders' of revolutions, either during their own lives or afterwards, often fighting against members of their very own community. The difference between them and their more ordinary contemporaries is, in my opinion, largely a matter of empowerment—and to question the source of that empowerment is to shed light on the importance of taking action.

The way in which individuals like Martin Luther King were empowered was in their realization that history is in the hands of individuals. Importantly, whatever one does, one shapes the history of humankind, and so inaction is as much a contribution to the future of one's community as action. In 1963, Dr. King said:

> ... [A] tragic misconception of time... [is] that there is something in the very flow of time that will inevitably cure all ills. Actually, time itself is neutral; it can be used either destructively or constructively.... Human progress never rolls in on wheels of inevitability; it comes through the tireless efforts of men...

Once an individual realizes that it is she who can create history, she is empowered and she can begin to be a truly responsible member of the human community. Martin Luther King also said, "...an individual who breaks a law that conscience tells him is unjust...is in reality expressing the highest respect for law." In other words, the greatest good one can do for humanity is in actuality questioning one's environment and letting one's conscience speak to oneself to the point that one feels compelled—largely for one's own self-respect and sense of responsibility—to take action. In this sense, self-questioning, the basis of all action, is as much a private responsibility—a matter of every individual's conscience—as it is a public responsibility. There is actually no separation between the private and public conscience, because from one stems the other.

But as Dr. King himself pointed out, there are good people in the world—who, one would think, have the security and the power to bring about change—who maintain an "appalling silence." Why is it that there are people who do not react to their conscience to the point of taking some kind of public action? In my opinion, the answer to this lies in education. Far from being encouraged to be intelligently risk-taking, children are actively taught to quell their natural instincts of questioning and seeking answers; they are actively taught to follow the voice of authority and to conform to what is generally popular. So, although many adults may privately feel dissatisfied about their environment, there are few adults who actually feel empowered enough to take action publicly. The idea of history as being brought about by the actions of individuals is virtually not taught to humans. It then becomes the added responsibility of those who decide to fight for change also to combat this problem. Indeed, most leaders fighting for change have also found themselves becoming gadflies, creating tension in society: this becomes an inevitable part of the battle for one's belief. But I think that leaders seeking justice in their communities should make it a point to educate children not necessarily in their beliefs but more importantly in the skills of questioning and reflection.

When one is fighting for change against the law in some way, or when one is fighting against the law itself in some way, then I believe that one's fight should be non-violent. I find the step-wise progression towards goals used by Martin Luther King and many others before him (such as M. K. Gandhi) intelligent and humane. The steps of *collection of facts*, *negotiation*, *self-purification*, and *direct action* ensure that the relationship between the self and one's opponents never turns mindlessly hostile. This is important, I feel, because it is important to understand one's opponents not just as in the wrong, but to understand how and why they are the way they are. If, as a leader, one thinks of oneself as an active agent in history, then one must understand the presumptive faults of one's opponents not as bad in themselves, but as the products of the history one is shaping. Non-violence, and subsequently a complete knowledge and understanding of one's context, also involves an acceptance of punishment, perhaps even punishment one does not agree with. Leaders such as Socrates and Martin Luther King, and even literary-mythic figures such as Sophocles' Antigone, demonstrated such an acceptance of punishment.

To conclude, the role of the individual in civilized society is one of responsibility, and as I said, this responsibility works on several levels, simultaneously addressing one's private identity and one's public identity, making them one and the same to a large extent. To be truly empowered means to realize the multiple meanings of one's responsibility, as an individual, and as a member of the human community.

Duality in Life and Reconciliation: The Death of Ivan Ilych

Sarah Kaslow

An individual with *DISSOCIATIVE identity disorder* (the psycho-pathology formerly known as *multiple personality disorder*) manifests two or more distinct identities or personality states. Each of these identities or personalities has its own relatively enduring pattern of perceiving, relating to, and thinking about the environment and the self. According to this definition, Leo Tolstoy might have asserted that everyone should be diagnosed with dissociative identity disorder. In many ways, we all suffer from two different types of lives: the artificial life and the authentic life. Furthermore, this duality is augmented by the duality of an inner life and an outer life.

The artificial life is one of superficial relationships, rampant self-interest, and unchecked materialism. Ivan Ilych becomes an example of how living in this way results in emptiness, isolation, dissatisfaction and decay; in a life incapable of providing answers to those questions of meaning that so desperately do need answers. How does one living a life of gross superficiality make sense of the end of life, of his relationships, projects, and dreams? How does one reconcile this way of life with the end of his very existence?

When the moment of death comes, one living the artificial life is able neither to find comfort in the strength of relationships built over the course of his life nor to take pride in anything concrete outside of himself. To realize this is crippling. When one uses relationships with others merely as a means to an end, he gains in the short run but suffers in the long run. By involving himself in relationships only to benefit himself, Ivan Ilych relates to others only in the shallowest way. While it may seem that this allows for the greater advance of his self-interests, this is not the case. In sacrificing potentially authentic relationships, Ivan sacrifices the more substantive gains of authenticity for the more immediate, but ultimately nearly worthless gains of artificiality. Paradoxically, authentic relationships provide *more* support insofar as one denies himself a measure of self-interest for the betterment of all involved, and, in so doing, becomes vastly more fulfilled.

The artificial life is a deception that hides life's true meaning and leaves one terrified and alone at the moment of death. In order to avoid this terror, one may—indeed an entire society may—maintain the pretense that death need never be acknowledged. In this false denial and avoidance of death, one can suspend any recognition of the superficiality of one's relationships, self-interest, and vapid acquisitiveness, and one thus defends himself from these unpleasant realities. The avoidance of death so prominent in Tolstoy's story demonstrates that Ivan's social milieu is based on a delusion designed to protect those who live artificial lives from the corrosive emptiness that will inexorably consume them.

In contrast to the artificial life, the authentic life is marked by pity and compassion for others. It sees others not as means to ends, but as individual beings with unique thoughts, feelings, and desires. The authentic life cultivates mutually affirming human relationships that break down isolation and allow for true interpersonal contact. The authentic life fosters strength through solidarity and comfort through empathy. It creates bonds and prepares one to meet death. The compassion and love of the authentic life are genuine and reciprocal. While helping another, one also benefits. In creating genuine relationships, one finds himself with a great deal of support in his last days on Earth and is more able to accept death. One living the authentic life is more able to recognize the realities of life, mainly its unpredictable nature. At the point of death, the authentic individual is self-assured, peaceful, and perhaps even joyous.

The dichotomy of an inner and outer life coincides with the artificial-authentic life dichotomy. Living to satisfy the outer life promotes pleasure and survival; utterly ignoring it invites physical suffering and death. Yet if one completely ignores or denies his inner wants, he will nonetheless experience excruciating pain, overwhelming unhappiness, and absolute terror. This is yet another perspective on *The Death of Ivan Ilych*. In denying his inner needs, Ivan is not capable of transcending the physical. It is easy to criticize him for mistaking his outer life for his true inner life, but at the same time it is often difficult to recognize the dualities in our own selves and to live a balanced life. Which life is the more important one to satisfy? How does one find a balance? More fundamentally, how do we tell the difference between our outer life and our inner life when, as is so often the case, the boundary seems hopelessly blurred?

If we are capable of recognizing our inner life, we are more capable of moving beyond our suffering, conquering the fear of death, and experiencing true joy. Perhaps, with Ivan Ilych as an example, it is impossible to completely reconcile our inner-outer life and authentic-artificial life dichotomies in a way other than death. The Tolstoy portrayal is strikingly similar to that in Kate Chopin's *The Awakening*. Recognizing the duality is difficult, but the character Edna "had apprehended instinctively the dual life—that outward existence which conforms, the inward life which questions." Reconciliation of these two lives, although she recognizes their separate existence, is impossible, and Edna meets a fate similar to Ivan's. We must then ask—and not rest until we have answered—*How are we different from these two?*

CUSTOMS AND EXPECTATIONS

Janice Claire Serrano Tan

READING *THE DEATH OF Ivan Ilych* was one of the most frustrating experiences that I have ever undergone. From the very beginning of the story, I realized that there was something terribly wrong with Ivan's life: it was meaningless. Ivan Ilych lived his life according to the superficial rules of society. He believed that he should work towards impressing others, and doing what society deemed proper. In short, Ivan Ilych led an 'ideal' life, according to society's standards. However, I firmly believe that this was a very, very grave mistake, and throughout the entire story, I felt a gnawing urge to stand up and shout, *"No, no, no! You've got it all wrong!"*

Am I refuting hundreds of years of societal development and progress by claiming society's expected conduct is detrimental to one's self? As daunting as it may seem, I must confess that, yes, I am stubbornly refusing to accept that the ideal life can be attained through following societal rules. I cannot help but feel that there is something intrinsically profound about a human life, and to try and limit the purpose of that valuable life to that of following societal customs just seems like an absurdly ridiculous waste.

However, I am not claiming that customs are completely detrimental to society. In fact, cultural customs instill a sense of community in those that practice them. I grew up with a mix of Chinese, Filipino and American influences, and thus I feel a sense of kinship with those who also practice those same conventions and beliefs.

These influences constitute a large part of who I am today, and yet there seems to be something infinitely more profound about my humanity that is acting as a driving force behind all these various influences. For instance, growing up with my Chinese father, I have always valued the importance of sharing food. If I were to refuse a hungry person food, it would to me be just as bad as physically harming them. However, the significance to me of sharing food is much more than a habit that I adopted from Chinese culture. It is the intention behind that custom which makes it significant. Chinese recognize food as essential to life, so sharing food with a fellow human being is similar to sharing one's blessings, as well as sustaining that person's life.

Perhaps the significance of customs is never completely the same for any two people, but they are still similar enough to create a bond between those two persons. This sense of kinship is something that I often feel towards various persons. In Manila, I often felt a sense of community with people who shared my Filipino belief of being an optimist and celebrating life. In fact, I dedicated a large portion of my International Baccalaureate Art portfolio towards this exemplary Filipino trait. I was not compelled to believe in optimism because it was a Filipino teaching, but it introduced me to the custom, and I was able to discern for myself whether or not the significance behind the custom was truly worthy of being practiced.

Ivan Ilych did not look beyond the outward purpose of his actions or into their underlying significance. He wanted to decorate his home according to what society views as 'pleasant,' and yet he did not realize that the purpose for this societal convention is to please others. Ivan Ilych decorated his home to impress others and heighten their esteem of him, but not to bring them or himself pleasure or happiness at seeing the beauty of his own home. He married his wife because it seemed to him to be the expected thing to do; however, he completely missed the significance of marriage. I personally believe that marriage is based on love; it is the affirmation of the love between two persons. In ancient China, arranged marriages may not have been based on love, but they were based on the merging of two families. If I had lived in ancient China and had had to marry a complete stranger, I may not have been as happy as I would be marrying in the present for love, but the marriage would not be any less significant were it instead driven by honor, filial piety and perhaps even a desire to experience a new chapter of life. One thing I cannot imagine is marrying for the sake of custom, and not for the underlying significance of that custom. This is the mistake that Ivan Ilych made, and it is a mistake that cost him his life.

Customs themselves are imperfect. Nowadays the concept of an arranged marriage or Chinese foot binding seems strange and unethical. I myself agree that they are unfair and have justly been abolished. However, though the customs themselves seem flawed, the significance of the custom is nonetheless important. I cannot say that an old woman who cannot walk because she has bound feet has meaninglessly lost her ability to work and empower herself. To her, bound feet do not merely imply deformed toes and painful arthritis, but rather they are symbolic of beauty, grace and commitment to community. Perhaps she wishes that she did not have bound feet for the practical consequences of impaired mobility, but the many virtues and meanings associated with her bound feet have made the experience meaningful. Therein lies an element of compensation—perhaps a decisive one.

This is why I avoid judging different cultures. When I first heard about the concept of hara-kiri, the Japanese ritual of honorary suicide, I was completely shocked at how this could possibly be a virtuous act. Clearly, I thought, this act devalues human life and is a completely brutal sort of obligation to impose upon anyone for any reason. I viewed hara-kiri as a disgusting degradation of human life that should be completely eliminated from Japanese culture. However, when I moved to the Philippines and attended the International School Manila where I made many Japanese friends, I noticed a sort of rigidness about some of them when it concerned virtue and honor. Many of my Japanese friends would joke about the wild fashion trends of modern Japanese youth; however, they were surprisingly serious on the topics of discipline and hara-kiri.

My friends explained to me that discipline and honor (which is the reason for committing hara-kiri) is a big part of Japanese culture, and I regret to admit that its underlying significance is something which I am not privy to because of my lack of exposure to that culture. I assume that it is something similar to my understanding of Chinese, Filipino or American culture. In fact, cultural conventions almost seem to have a certain qualia which members of other cultures are not privy to. For instance, when I am explaining the significance of food based on my Chinese upbringing, I still feel as if there is a certain aspect of my understanding which I am unable to fully explain. When reading Confucius, Pearl S. Buck or Amy Tan, I often have a sort of intrinsic understanding of the significance of their accounts of Chinese culture. It is a lie for me to say that I agree with all of Confucius's teachings, especially his belief that it is better to study than to innovate, and yet there are many things which he says, such as his description of a gentleman, where I say to myself, "My goodness, that makes perfect sense!" This leads me to the question: are there people who would agree with aspects of Confucianism and Chinese culture that I disagree with? Who is more correct, me or them? If I had grown up in their situation, would I also agree with their beliefs, even the belief that studying is better than innovation?

First of all, I do not want to get too carried away with my justification of different beliefs. I believe first and foremost that we have an intrinsic sense of morality, so things like murder, theft and cruelty are obviously wrong. However, when it comes to things like hara-kiri, the act itself may seem wrong, but the significance behind the act is utterly, completely, dead-on right. When my friend explained to me the concept of hara-kiri, I was able to understand it because the sense of honor that it fiercely upholds is similar to that in Chinese culture. Individuals commit hara-kiri in order to prove their innocence, and/or preserve their honor. For instance, politicians who are accused of corruption would commit hara-kiri to prove their innocence because they are showing that they value honor and integrity over their own life, thus it is impossible that they would compromise it for material gain. And though I am against suicide because I fervently believe in the preciousness of human life, there is still something in the significance of hara-kiri with which I empathize.

This creates a dilemma for me. Should I condone an unethical act because its underlying significance is paramount to a culture's qualia? Or should I reject a custom simply because a certain act is unacceptable? Ivan Ilych, if he ever got around to asking himself these questions, would most likely choose to reject alien customs. I, however, must be a little more careful in my considerations because, as I have realized from my experience in an international community, cultural identity is of massive significance to most persons. It is certainly very important to me.

In fact, if my parents were not Asian, but instead another race, would I still love them as much as I do now? I am confident that I would continue to love them no matter what, but it would definitely be very awkward for me if I did not have a cultural connection with them. However, I believe that the connection brought about by genuine compassion and love is much stronger than that of cultural understanding. Perhaps I would never get used to eating foreign foods, instead wishing for more familiar Chinese, Filipino or American meals, but because I care about them, I would eat anything for the sake of their comfort.

A few months ago I attended a Christian church, and the pastor preached that it would be difficult to marry someone of a different faith because your goals, priorities, etc. would be completely different. This is also how I feel about culture. People of different cultural backgrounds would have a harder time interacting with each other, just as I've always felt like the odd one out amongst a group of Japanese girls at the International School. First, there is the obvious problem of the language barrier.

Second, there is the problem of comfort. People feel more comfortable around those with similar beliefs because they can predict their behavior better.

However, I think that cultural differences must take a back seat to human love and affection. I love my parents and brother first and foremost, and whether or not I share the same culture or beliefs would not change my devotion to them. This conclusion is of paramount importance to my life. It is the source of my strength and happiness. Whenever I am in an awful situation, I realize that I have something infinitely wonderful in my life that I should be happy for: my family. Indeed, I have attempted to write a *Civilization* essay on a topic other than family, yet I have inevitably strayed right back to my family.

So focusing back on the question at hand: do societal customs and expectations make life less meaningful, or are they essential to living a significant life? Yes, societal customs may make life meaningful, as long as one understands and believes in the significance of a custom, and is not merely carrying out the custom because it was dictated to them. However, a meaningful life does not even require societal customs. All that you need to live a meaningful life is a person you love so much that it is impossible to comprehend.

I am very grateful to have three of them. Thank you, Mom, Dad and Daniel.

A COMMON UNDERSTANDING

Hunter Jackson

IN *THE STRUCTURE OF Scientific Revolutions*, Thomas Kuhn shows how science furthers itself by conducting experiments that generally affirm or build upon existing scientific paradigms. By doing this, science can successfully avoid the paradigm shifts that create the discomfort inherent in major change. The same principles can be applied to the way humans cling to the beliefs with which we feel comfortable, and generally do not change easily. Throughout history, debates and discussions have followed a round-about pattern that, more often than not, leads to no resolution between the two sides of a problem. During the semester, however, I have worked to scrutinize and to adapt my fundamental beliefs, and tried to avoid the brick wall that hard-held beliefs often pose to change. Questioning my intel-lectually based conviction that our existence is self-decided and that the universe has no namable deity, for example, has been one of the most prodigious mental tasks I have ever undertaken; however, only by constantly challenging my conceptions of the world, have I been able to discover a middle ground between atheism and evangelicalism, where a non-physical interiority that cannot be explained or mapped by scientific processes exists.

At the year's beginning, I believed that there was no god or destiny controlling our lives, and that only we have the power to control it. This has not entirely changed. However, throughout the year I have also deeply debated whether or not there exists some kind of universal non-physical interiority to the world—something I shall henceforth call *coherence* because it is presumably felt by all humans. I have juggled a belief similar to Freud's that religion is only a comforting mass delusion with the idea that the Cartesian notion of *res extensa* is alone not sufficient to describe our existence. After examining both, and trying to make sure that I was not simply avoiding the cognitive dissonance that can come with existentialism, I came to the conclusion that there is some sort of coherent force beyond our control. This, I believe, is demonstrated by the sacrifice of oneself to help a stranger, the missing of an old friend or lover, or the drive to do good or bad. How can these things be explained? Granted, there are arguments based on evolution, chemical processes, and other physical forces for these activities. By itself though, I do not believe that science or physical descriptions can completely describe these occurrences. I think that forces that drive us to such not necessarily orderly and often totally unpredictable behaviors have to exist in the world. These forces represent the coherence in our universe. They can affect any human, even though they are not themselves predictable or mapped in any way. It is because of forces like these, that I share Tolstoy's belief that a world defined only by science is a cold and incomplete place.

The construction of my conception of coherence above required the rattling of my previous beliefs of existentialism and disorder, and is still only minutely developed. Our beliefs determine how we view the world, and any change in our most profound religious beliefs, or lack thereof, can violently disturb the truth as we know it. For example, if one were to challenge the existentialist concept of a self-decided existence, the existentialist would be forced to uproot or at least put into question the life he had been living so far. If he earnestly took the oppositions argument into consideration, then he would have to consider whether the choices he thought he had been making his entire life were really his choices at all.

Four factors in psychology help to explain why we so tenaciously cling to our beliefs. The first two, belief bias and confirmation bias, state that we view the world in such a way that confirms our preexisting beliefs. For example, an atheist would look at famine as evidence of godlessness, while a Christian may look at famine as retribution for man's wickedness. The third psychological factor is belief perseverance, which states that human's have the tendency to cling to and argue for beliefs even if they are given direct proof of the falsity of these beliefs. The fourth and final factor is cognitive dissonance. This states that discomfort is felt when our values or usual perspective on the world are contradicted, and we adapt our thoughts and behaviors to control it. The unwillingness to change or give up ground on a certain subject that results from these factors, leads to the circular pattern of discussion that is witnessed in philosophy, diplomacy, business, and many other scenarios in which one side is arguing against another. This problem causes more than mere standstills in that it severely limits our capacity ultimately to find the truth within our universe. Freud, Descartes, Aristotle and Socrates all developed their paramount works by challenging every viewpoint, and changing those they found to be incorrect or incomplete. In *A Discourse on Method*, Descartes speaks of the piecewise manner in which he developed his conceptions of truth. He started with the simplest hypothesis, and only moved on to the next more complicated one when he was sure of its essential consonance with the facts of the world. Thus he constructs his famous *cogito*: "I think therefore I am." The pursuit of truth is not based on the refusal to give up a blind axiom. It is based, rather, on the development and scrutiny of all ideas, and most importantly, the willingness to change an idea if it is disproved or insupportable.

I still have the belief that no god exists in our universe, and no universal order of the sort typically defined by religion is anything more than false. Nevertheless, I have been drawn at least slightly toward a middle ground, a compromise where I acknowledge *res cogitans* next to a much larger belief in the physical and scientific in our world. It can be said that I have not actually changed my beliefs, and I have not given up much on the subject of existentialism. This is partly true. I have only begun to try and examine the world without preconceptions and biases, and still cling to many. But by relentlessly challenging my own beliefs and allowing myself to move, if only the smallest amount, towards the center of the two poles of religion that philosophers have struggled with since the beginning, and that other class members and I have struggled with all semester, I have been able to adapt and slightly modify one of the vertebrae of the backbone of my beliefs. I cannot say how concrete this compromise is; only by continuing to experience the world can I completely develop it. Without a willingness to challenge and possibly to change a belief, however, neither I, nor anybody else, will ever be able to truthfully describe and understand the universe that we live in.

THE VALUE OF HUMAN LIFE

Lauren Thompson

DOES ONE'S CIVILIZATION HAVE the right or duty to intervene in another civilization's affairs (at least under certain circumstances)? What could justify such intervention?

In his November 2nd "Rally the Vote" speech in Dallas, Texas, President George W. Bush made this solemn pledge to the American people: "Over the next four years, I will continue to stand for the values that are important to our nation... I stand for a culture of life in which every person matters and every being counts." Throughout history America has shown that it is dedicated to protecting and maintaining the sanctity of human life. From our intervention in both World Wars to Korea, Vietnam, and currently in the Middle East, America has fought to supplant fascism, communism, and terrorism (all ideologies that suppress the human spirit) with democracy—the universal vehicle for freedom, liberty, and peace. This country has worked tirelessly and selflessly to defeat the evil that perpetrated the Nazi concentration camps, Stalinist gulags, Vietnamese torture camps, and the senseless murdering of innocents by Saddam Hussein and al-Qaeda (to which the recently discovered mass graves and the events of September 11th can attest, respectively). To paraphrase Secretary of State Colin Powell: "America has fought in [the aforementioned] wars and asked only for the ground to bury her dead." Behind the evil incarnate that is manifest in these forms of utter violence, America really fights to uphold the great worth that can be found in every human life. What has been confused for decades with imperialist greed is nothing more than this country's sincere belief in and adherence to freedom. Although speaking decades apart, Presidents Reagan and W. Bush were motivated by the same precept when famously declaring (respectively): "Mr. Gorbachev, tear down this wall!" and "Our Nation, this generation, will lift a dark threat of violence from our people and our future. We will rally the world to this cause, by our efforts and by our courage. We will not tire, we will not falter, and we will not fail." To these Presidents and to America, freedom is not a select way of life for the fortunate but rather the inherent right of every human being: a gift derived from God.

As an American I do believe that one civilization has the right to intervene in another's affairs on behalf of the dignity of human life and the right to freedom. In the case of North and South Vietnam in the 1950s-60s, when the North Vietnamese dictator Ho Chi Minh began purging entire classes of people in the pursuit of a unified communist state, I believe it was the duty of the United States to aid President Diem's fledgling democracy in the South. The wide-scale violent suppression of the human spirit (via genocide or other means) and man's God-given right to freedom were, are, and always will be cause enough for a nation to intervene in another country's systematic, brutal repression of any segment of its population.

How does Graham Greene use Fowler, Pyle, and Phuong as a metaphor for the Western intervention in Indo-China in the 1950s?

Although an intense novel about the detrimental effect of innocence on society, Graham Greene's *Quiet American* is primarily an explication of the Vietnam War with regard to the involvement of the European and American powers. Personified by the character Fowler, old Europe, despite having occupied Vietnam for fifty years (via France), insists that it is not "engaged" in the struggle. This attitude of passivity and detachment permeates the plot and is reflected in Fowler's actions: the character insists that he has no ties to Vietnam, not even any emotional investments. When questioned by Captain Trouin, Fowler exclaims, "That's [the war's] no concern of mine. I'm not involved." When the Captain continues, "One day something will happen … you will take a side," Fowler emphatically states, "No, I'm going back to England" even though he has no such plans. Thus Fowler (Europe) appears an indecisive character, one not willing to take a moral stand but at the same time not willing to relinquish control––the care of Vietnam—to the United States. Fowler remains skeptical and somewhat jealous of Pyle, who represents America, and continually mocks his innocent optimism. To Fowler and Europe, democracy in Indo-China is viewed as an unattainable goal, and those who seek such a "utopia" are deemed either dense or foolish, or both. Thus Fowler does not feel any sympathy for Pyle when he is murdered, and his resentment is evident: "They killed him because he was too innocent to live. He was young and ignorant and silly and he got involved. He never saw anything he hadn't heard in a lecture hall, and his writers made a fool of him… [He was] a red menace, a soldier of democracy." In diametric opposition to Fowler's cynicism and general inaction, Pyle actively pursues a plan that he is convinced will help the Vietnamese people. Believing that a Third Force will bring both peace and justice to the region, Pyle seeks out General Thé and even involves himself in various civilian bombings in the support of his cause. As communicated by Fowler's (Europe's) incessant mockery of Pyle (America), the author's clear message is that although Pyle ostensibly has Phuong's (Vietnam's) "interests" at heart, his misguided ideology and naïveté ultimately result in a destructive end. This is further supported by Pyle's violent and painful murder, which although tragic, is neither outwardly mourned nor regretted by Fowler or Phuong. Greene allows Fowler to admit that he is "sorry" in the very last line of the novel, but it is never clear whether the Englishman regrets his own conduct or if he is truly sorry for Pyle. Perhaps it is actually Phuong for whom he is sorry, and rightfully so: in the end, Europe (i.e. France) and America abandoned Vietnam with the predictable result of massive purging and years of torture in the re-education camps for the South Vietnamese. Saigon is no more, but rather Ho Chi Minh's City mocks the more-than-50,000 American deaths. As was feared in the Domino Theory, when Vietnam fell to communism so did other regions in Indo-China; less than two decades later, the Khmer Rouge in Cambodia headed by Pol Pot murdered over 3 million people in short order as the world stood by.

THE MIXED CHILD

Maria Paredes

IN *TO KILL A Mockingbird,* by Harper Lee, Mayella Ewell is seen as a malevolent person, but she is just another mockingbird whose soul has been killed by society. I believe human nature is benign, but once humans commence to form societies and to seek power, the goodness of humans can be distorted, as it is in the case of Mayella. Mayella is the victim of the stereotypes, prejudices, and her father. Therefore her potential to do good is corrupted by the negative surroundings in which she lives, and this drives her to accuse Tom Robinson.

In this painting, titled *The Mixed Child*, Mayella and one of her younger brothers are portrayed as Maycomb's society sees them. Maycomb can only see the superficial and tangible aspects of the Ewells' lives; thus, this societal attitude makes them the subject of prejudice. Prejudice does not allow society to see the true identity of each individual. The setting of this painting is in Mayella's house.

She sits patiently waiting, while the sun sets. Every sunset is significant to Mayella because it signals the approach of the only contact she has with the real world: Tom Robinson. Mayella is isolated from society because of the prejudice of the Maycomb community. As Scout says, "She was as sad…as what Jem called a mixed child: white people wouldn't have anything to do with her because she lived among pigs; Negroes wouldn't have anything to do with her because she was white. She could not live with Mr. Dolphus Raymond, who prefers the company of Negroes, because she didn't own a river bank, and she wasn't from a fine old family…Maycomb gave them Christmas baskets, welfare, money, and the back of its hand." Maycomb cannot see the true identity of Mayella, and thus in the painting her face and the face of her small brother are blank to signify that even though society tries to take care of its people, it only offers them tangible things, while the power of stereotypes deprives them of an identity.

The Mixed Child. © 2005 Maria Paredes. Reprinted with permission.

CREATION, HERE AND THERE

Alex Ristow

FEW WOULD DISPUTE THAT religion has catalyzed some of history's most gruesome chapters: the Crusades, the Thirty Years' War, and the Holocaust all originated, at least in part, from religious tension. Unfortunately, religious conflicts stem from divergences far more deeply-rooted than those that arise from different pantheons of gods or disparate creation stories; some sets of beliefs are based on abstract foundations so dissimilar that reconciliation seems nearly impossible. The colonization of the Americas presents a perfect example of this type of religious incompatibility: European Christianity approached religion from a drastically different perspective then did the animism of the New World. In response to life's mysteries, one side presented a monotheistic, absolute, and comparatively disconnected God, while the other believed in a variety of gods or spirits that were inextricably connected to the natural world. Though it would appear, at least in the United States of America, that the Christian approach to life has overcome the Native American perspective, one could argue that the basic conflict between these sets of beliefs lives on in the modern clash between science and religion.

As a foundational text, *Genesis* provides both Christians and Jews with a somewhat abstract religious base. In this depiction of creation, God creates light, darkness, heaven, and earth simply by decreeing their existence; there is no manual shaping of the world or physical act of separating night and day. Furthermore, the Judeo-Christian God passes clear judgment on his creation, simply declaring the goodness of light and living creatures. In this sense, *Genesis* illustrates creation as an abstract process, one with a clear purpose and moral value in the eyes of God, but not necessarily an action whose motives humans can understand. The certainty with which God creates and judges his work, aided by the inflexibility of a written, as opposed to an oral, tradition, gives the Judeo-Christian religion a sense of absolutism and strict order. Throughout *Genesis* there exists almost no impression of a deep connection between men, animals, and earth—at least not a connection with the same intimacy that exists in animistic traditions. Men are linked with God through their form, but they are superior to the animals and disconnected from the earth. As evidence of their superiority, men are given dominion over the animals; as evidence of their less-than-intimate connection with the earth, Adam and Eve are cast out of Eden where nature becomes a source of labor, strife, and even fear. The story of *Genesis* clearly illustrates the Judeo-Christian belief that mankind's primary relationship is with God rather than the earth.

In contrast to the ideas of creation presented in *Genesis*, a variety of Native American tales represent the beginning of existence in a less absolute, more intimate way. Instead of creation through a decree, the earth is often shaped or molded physically, whether through stomping, dancing, tearing, or building. The world itself is portrayed as a nurturing mother figure, often a preexisting goddess or other form whose origin is not questioned. The fluidity of the Native American oral tradition also seems to allow for more uncertainty and speculation than does the Judeo-Christian text; as shown in Jamie de Angulo's dialogue, Native American storytellers are aware that every retelling of every story is subtly different. But despite differing accounts and even completely different stories between regions, many motifs run clearly throughout Native American accounts of creation. Foremost among these similarities is the idea of the connection between man and nature. Whereas in the Judeo-Christian tradition animals are viewed as lesser beings than men, in some American Indian tales animals are actually responsible for the creation of the earth. Man is not involved in an epic struggle against nature; instead, both are integral parts of an interconnected and intimate cycle of life. The earth itself possesses an anthropomorphic form: water springs from the goddess's eyes and mouth, plants from her hair and skin, and mountains from her shoulders and nose. Furthermore, when gods, spirits, or "Holy Ones" do appear in Native American stories, they do not pass judgment or make decrees but instead build, shape, and mold with their hands and bodies. Native American tradition clearly emphasizes the role of nature in connecting man's world with the spirit world; in fact, all three, nature, man, and spirit, are inextricably linked in a codependent relationship.

The distinctive cultures of the Native Americans and the Europeans initially came into contact in 1492 C.E. when Christopher Columbus stumbled upon the New World; however, the foundational struggle between the beliefs each culture represents has continued into the modern era. In America's largely Christian society, adherence to the Bible and to the absolute word of God remains a priority in the lives of many people. However, modern science has produced many contradictions to Biblical "facts" concerning the age, shape, location, and motion of the Earth. Therefore, while there are some who still promote a literal translation of their respective religious texts in all respects, there are citizens of all religions who now choose to believe in the observations and deductions of scientists. In a conceptual way, this conflict dates back to the clash between Native American and Judeo-Christian tradition. The question remains: are humans a small part of nature's all-encompassing whole or the superior beings in God's unknowable plan? The answer, it seems, may eternally remain unique to each country, culture, and individual.

Purpose-Driven Beings

Grady Wieger

LIFE IS A PRECIOUS gift that must be revered as fragile and as a formula worthy of substantial introspection. There is a reason we are all here on this earth, and every individual must face the reality that the short time spent living is to be used for good. The days of existence are given to us neither so that we can live in endless happiness nor so that we can be devoid of energy and excitement. There is an Odyssean middle ground (a balance) between the two extremes where we can have fun while using our talents to affect others. As stated by Thomas Carlyle, "The man without a purpose is like a ship without a rudder—a waif, a nothing, a no man." There is a purpose for life, and it is our duty to find that reason within ourselves. An orderly existence can be obtained by discovering your personal purpose for living; by looking to yourself, to others, and to God, you can find the reason within each breath you take.

Living solely for your desires, pleasures, and well-being brings about a skewed perspective of the world and of the meaning of life. When you live for yourself, you have no responsibilities to others, thus, you have no true responsibilities. When other people are involved in your life and can hold you accountable for your actions, you have a tendency to be more concerned with the relationships you have and how well they are bound. Without these connections, a man becomes stranded on an island of self-ishness with no way to reach the outside world. As a mark of immaturity, seeking personal pleasure in all that is done brings about unhealthy behavior resulting in personal downfall. Men should not act like children (emotionally immature beings that are unable to see deeper into the meaning of existence) for the entirety of their lives. We are not designed to remain children. We are designed to grow up and to mature into purpose-driven creatures. Being devoid of pain or suffering is, paradoxically, dangerous and another sign of emotional immaturity. Mistakes and tragedies build character and a better understanding of life on a broad scale. Life's fragility can be placed within a better perspective when misfortune is juxtaposed with prosperity. When a person wishes to ignore all pain and only find pleasure in the enticing obsessions the world has to offer in infinite forms, danger lurks. Life has no depth or meaning when it is solely measured by your own standards of good and amusement. It is the incorporation of the misfortunes, opinions, and guidance of others that adds an invaluable insight to one's meaning.

Humans are creatures of community; we need others both to lean on when we are faced with challenges or heartaches and to share our exuberance when we experience times of great joy. Therefore, living a life focused on our relationships with others is key to a good life. Offer yourself as a servant within and beyond those relationships, for, as it states in Mark 10:43, "Whoever wants to be great must become a servant." This does not mean that you must offer yourself as a slave or present yourself as someone who can be taken advantage of, but that you give yourself up as a helper, a giver, and a friend. Make it your responsibility to make a difference in the life of someone else, even if it is via the performance of some small, seemingly insignificant task. Life's minute details are often overlooked, but the opportunities that arise in a moment's passing make the biggest difference in the lives of all who are affected. When you help others, a sense of personal satisfaction comes with the action, but this is not something to be ashamed of. This satisfaction can be used to fill the place of the pleasure that comes with acting on selfish desires. Lending a helping hand spreads an awareness of relationships and goodness. It causes people to look beyond themselves and to ask the question, "What can I do for you?" Although existing for the benefit of others is a sure sign of emotional maturity, one must not lose sight of the personal necessities of health it takes to endure life's chaos. You must take care of yourself while maintaining the focus on others.

The balance between fulfilling personal necessity and devoting oneself to others brings new depth and meaning to existence. As illustrated by Leo Tolstoy in *The Death of Ivan Ilych*, life's fragility cannot be overlooked. Ivan did not attain the balance of relationships and self while he had the chance, and his self-examination while lying on his deathbed only proves the uncertainty of his purpose. Ivan asks himself the question of existence as his life draws to a close, "but however much he ponder[s] the question, he [finds] no answer." Ivan is too late to discover the purpose of his life, and his struggle over whether he has lived as he should have further reveals his doubts about life's meaning. A lifetime of self-satisfaction, self-gratification and conformance to empty convention has turned him away from his family and any other authentic connections. The lesson is clear: when life is lived as an individual and not as part of a true community, suffering is inevitable.

Moved by this story and the discussions in our *Questions of Civilization* class, I have begun my own search for my purpose in life. A drive to deepen my understanding of myself, others, and God more fervently asserts itself than it ever has in my past. I have taken it upon myself to find and uphold this balance between service and enjoyment that I have explained. Never before have I asked the "big" questions of life. Quite frankly, I have never had the desire or interest to ask those questions. But with all of the changes I have experienced through leaving home, coming to college, meeting new people, and questioning myself, I have found the desire to search for my place within the greater community known as humanity. I now think about what I want to do, who I want to be, and what I want to live for. I know that I exist for God and all that He embodies, for my family and friends, and for those that I do not yet know but whom I will eventually come into contact with. It is this focus on others that I want to uphold throughout my life. I know that there will be trying times that will test my strength, but with the help of God, I can continue to touch lives even through my weaknesses. As humans, it is our obligation to question ourselves from a multitude of perspectives. We must seek the purpose that has been given to each of us, and use our individual talents to fulfill that purpose within the time allotted by God. The meaning of life is beyond ourselves no matter how hard we try to redirect its focus on our own desires and pleasures. Therefore, we must interact with others to discover the hidden details within the greater experience we call life. Strive to be a representation of the strong balance between yourself, others, and God in all that you do so that you may become a model of existence to all who witness your actions.

EVER-EVOLVING ELINOR

Maria Santos

> *"In her first passion woman loves her lover;*
> *in all the others, all she loves is love."*
> —Byron, *Don Juan III*

I BELIEVE THAT EVERYBODY wants to fall in love at some point. I certainly crave human connection and intimacy whether it is through a touch, conversation, or even a kiss. Without this connection to other human beings, I would feel isolated, withdrawn, and lonesome. In order to fall in love with a person, I must expose my vulnerability. As a pragmatist, much like Elinor in *Sense and Sensibility*, I hesitate to allow others (especially males) to become too close to me. I believe in protecting and defending myself. My mother always tells me, "You must protect yourself because no one else will." I realize that I am alone in this world and I am responsible for my physical and emotional well-being. I maintain self-preservation by possessing a hard exterior along with various defense mechanisms. However, I do struggle a great deal with the notion of potentially shutting people out of my life. This idea is very frightening for me, and eliminating loved ones from my life is far from my actual intention. At times I feel that I am too harsh, but never foolish. In essence, I would rather a man see me as emotionally strong and independent rather than weak and dependent. Also, I am not a very trusting person. I believe that everyone is fallible. Everyone has weaknesses and temptations. What separates people of a higher, more respectable moral code is whether they surrender to those weaknesses and temptations or not.

Indeed I exhibit a superposition of certain principles concerning love. I am definitely a young woman who deprives herself of certain luxuries and indulgences, namely exhibiting outward passions—much like Elinor. Of course I have the capacity to be emotionally affected by someone or something, but there are many times when I choose not to be. I do not want one man to be my reason for living, because I live for self-fulfillment, to achieve my goals and dreams. I would not tell a man that he is my reason for living, because he is not. A part of me is admittedly saddened by this hardened view that I have consciously chosen to adopt. As a child, I was emotionally sensitive. I was naive and trusting. I never thought that a person so close to me could hurt me, but he did. (I am speaking of my father). Now I realize that those closest to me have the capacity to do the most harm. Ever since my father betrayed me, my vision of men and relationships has been skewed. No matter how much somebody tells you he loves you, he is nonetheless capable of being devious and subject to temptation. With this, I am more than willing to protect my own feelings and not to display them. I do not feel that it is necessary to profess my love to someone because I convey my affections through actions, namely maternal actions. I want to take care of those I love.

My defense mechanisms will eventually be nothing but destructive to a romantic relationship. My partner would feel that I am insensitive, aloof, uncaring, and calculating. The truth is that I am a young woman who has been internalizing my problems since adolescence. I, again like Elinor, internally invest my senses with great depth and meaning. I do not let my feelings be known, for fear of being taken advantage of. I grapple with this issue of presenting myself as too harsh because I know that relationships involve self-sacrifice, but at the same time I value my selfish, self-absorbed ways. I fear someone getting in the way of my dreams. I have one life to live an incredible adventure. Why should I let someone stop me? I fear that once a man knows I would live and die for him, he will betray me, with the security that I will never leave him. I feel much more stable when I practice pragmatism, restraint, and even apathy. Presenting myself in this manner provides me with a sense of control. I believe having such forethoughts is healthy.

A true romantic risks a great deal of emotional battery and abuse because she (or he) idealizes her loved ones. She places them on a pedestal and elevates them to a God-like status, and this often skews her vision of both the beloved and the relationship. To the romantic, her partner is not capable of any wrongdoing. Romantics are often in love with the concept of love itself, with the idea of being "high" on another person, and so become unable to distinguish reality from fantasy in their relationships. They sometimes will deny that an injustice has occurred. I do not want to be the victim of a romantic relationship, especially since I do not believe that it is the most important thing life has to offer.

Obviously, having a romantic relationship is one way to have a fulfilling life, but I realize that there are other ways to feel fulfilled as a human being: pursuing an education, focusing on career goals, learning a new skill, or rearing a family are just some of the wonderful paths life has to offer. I do not think there is one chief element of importance to life; rather, many balanced components make up a satisfying life. Also, I do not believe in the idea of "love at first sight," which is clearly exemplified by Marianne: within ten minutes of meeting John Willoughby, she has fallen in love. I believe that two people can be attracted to one another, but there is no immediate basis for love. Love also takes many different forms. For instance, no matter how wonderful a man is to me, I could never love him the same way I love my mother. I do not think I can love someone more than her. I also believe that no man would sacrifice as much as my mother does to give me the best life. My mother's love is unconditional, whereas a man's love can very well be conditional.

Also, I have a responsibility to my family, especially my parents, to choose an appropriate romantic partner, which is part of the Confucian notion of filial piety. I want my partner to understand and embrace my family. It is my duty to not be rebellious against my parents. They have given me life and have shown me love. They are always encouraging and supporting me to be the best individual I can be; therefore, I must respect their judgment and advice.

By possessing a true knowledge of how to govern my feelings, I can achieve a more balanced life. Marianne's deep sorrows and joys only bring her to points of ecstasy, which are far from stable. Leading a life of moderation will lead me to fulfillment and happiness. I feel the need to abandon my once sensitive feelings and guard myself, even though at times I feel tempted to let my guard down. I feel it is my duty to maintain reason, restraint, social responsibility, insight, and judgment. I have the tendency to get emotional easily, but have developed the restraint to do so only rarely. Marianne's impulsive candor is not well respected in the professional world. If I were to play the Marianne in a law firm, I would soon be dubbed the "Drama Queen!" Women have been stereotyped as emotional for centuries. I do not want to contribute to this generalization. I want to maintain a sense of logic to my romantic views.

However, a part of me concurs with Freud when he writes in *Civilization and Its Discontents*, "It is not easy to deal scientifically with feelings." It is difficult to constantly suppress my sentiments. I have this conflict that sometimes I want to feel as if I have no responsibility for anyone or anything. Sometimes I want to be irrational and less controlled. At times, I yearn to be spontaneous and impulsive with love, but I know that is foolish and idealistic. At times I want to profess my rapturous devotion to my boyfriend, but I merely entertain the thought. I find that one of the reasons I involve myself in a romantic relationship is to take care of another human being, to work my maternal instincts. I tend to show my affection for people by taking care of them.

The aspect of Marianne I can best relate to is that she never seems satisfied. I am always thinking of new ways to improve myself and the people around me. I wonder if there is a man out there who can keep up with my evolutionary process! According to Freud, our relations with others constitute one cause for our unhappiness. I agree with Freud to the extent that when we love deeply, we run the great risk of experiencing deep pain and sorrow. However, I know that relations with others can also bring me great joy. The thought of letting my guard down is daunting, but it also may be a positive change. No doubt it will take a long time to open up completely to my partner. When I find myself considering my boyfriend in future scenarios, I feel like the foolish romantic that Marianne is. At the same time, I feel happy and hopeful during those moments. One thing I will not sacrifice is my happiness. This leads me to the recognition that my inner Elinor has been transformed—not radically, but just enough so that I can maintain the creative, romantic passion that I miss when I long to be Marianne. I will be a better partner and overall woman if I embrace Marianne more. She inspires me to relieve my anxieties and to find the inner peace to trust others.

LIFE LESSONS

Maria Santos

"What is lovely never dies, but passes into other loveliness."
–Thomas Bailey Aldrich, *A Shadow of the Night*

THERE HAVE BEEN SEVERAL recent instances in which I hesitated to pass judgment on others, and it has worked beautifully, for it aided in my character development of compassion and understanding. The beauty in not judging others is followed by an impending development of accepting others and finding inner peace.

I walked into his room for the first time as merely his "friend." After the sufficiently awkward silence, I noticed the pained look on his face and we both began to cry. We cried for hours. I was finally able to witness firsthand all of the destruction I had caused in someone else's life. I had no intention of causing so much pain to a certain individual. It seemed as if I had killed a part of him, and I could not judge him for feeling a particular way about me. Also, I could not judge him for his vulnerable manner, since I had provoked that. He admitted to me that he had finally found what he was looking for in a companion; however, I was just embarking on my personal journey. I told him that he would find happiness again, but he was very skeptical. What caused my tears was that I had difficulty accepting my own cruelness: how I led someone to believe I was more serious than I actually was. Of course, hurting him was far from my actual intention. I had come to the realization that since we were taking separate paths in life, it would never work between us. I apologized for my selfish desire to be in a relationship, but I knew my apology was not enough. Now, my actions must reflect the type of soul searching that I intend to embark on. Relationships, whether romantic or platonic, are sacred institutions. I have realized that I cannot have everything I want. Knowing that I have hurt someone else pains me to no end. I do not regret our experiences together because they have taught me a great deal about myself, and I am glad to have provided him with resilience and strength. When I am invested in a relationship, I put my heart and soul into it because I want it to succeed. I simply ran out of energy, and had no time for myself to reflect on what I wanted from my own life. I wish our relationship could have been more platonic and casual, because it would have been less daunting and demanding for me. The demands of a serious relationship were far too much for me to handle. However, I owed it to him to be completely honest that I needed to be free to find myself. Suddenly, he was becoming such a large part of my identity, and the most daunting consideration for me was not having the time to fully craft an identity of my own.

In Mary Wollstonecraft's *Vindication of the Rights of Women*, she states that the "desire of pleasing men will grow languid." I was tired of being a servant and a mother to him. Of course I wanted to be the perfect companion for him, but I was damaging myself in the process. I was emotionally drained by having to hold our relationship together. I was the anchor: the student, the daughter, the sister, the girlfriend, the mother, the worker, the initiator, and the caretaker. I always admired a person of versatility (my mother comes to mind), but I had too many roles to assume at one time. He did not seem to grasp the permanence of my desire to be free. I told him I needed my freedom for as long as I could have it. I want to sit down and read about the world and its people. I want to find my place in society. I want to wander and walk alone. I believe that this will make me a better young woman because I will have spent quality time with myself. By spring break, I had found myself practically married to Jane Austen's Mr. Woodhouse from *Emma*—in a condition of virtual stasis—and my life was proceeding on a simplistic, common path. This is exactly the opposite of what I wanted! No longer will I damage others; rather, I will repair myself by combating my own inner demons and vices. The *Bhagavad-Gita* reminds me in the Seventh Teaching that, "divine traits of fearlessness, determination, honesty, absence of anger, peace, compassion for creatures, and clarity will lead to freedom." I must place my diligence in the development of these divine traits, which will foster my personal growth. According to the *Gita*, talking with my former boyfriend was a form of verbal penance for myself, in which I was able to be honest without offending him, all while providing him with a sense of comfort and compassion. Following the verbal penance was mental penance, in which I was able to find peace of mind while clarifying my feelings and desires. The *Bhagavad-Gita* also holds that mental penance encompasses several things: serenity, silence, self-restraint, and purity of being. After accepting my actions and offering him my apology, I felt completely calm. I also felt liberated, as if a heavy load were lifted from my shoulders.

When I think about the next stage our relationship will take, I am reminded of a particular Mary Wollstonecraft quote, "In the course of nature, friendship or indifference succeeds love," meaning that love simply is not enough to hold a relationship together. There must be another element of depth that is impossible to be removed from the foundation of the relationship. There was no basis or core to our romantic relationship; to our detriment we had never been friends prior to it. I did not know him well enough. In essence, I did not take my time with getting to see many aspects of his being. Wollstonecraft affirms that, "A woman can only be the friend or the slave of a man." At this time, I will be a friend to any man, but I must be a slave to no one but myself, pleasing myself and fulfilling my needs. I cannot serve another person the way I would want to serve myself right now. I am aware that since social relationships are the glue that holds societies together, loneliness and social isolation can easily serve as a threat to societal solidarity. I do not want to be alone forever. However, I believe that this is a crucial developmental stage in my life, and I must take advantage of it. However, I know that life is filled with progressions and changes. Our relationship is unique because we have now taken a step back, and are ready to know each other as people, and not as romantic partners. There is a great deal of irony involved when your romantic partner suddenly assumes the role of your friend. I truly feel that we were meant to be good friends and nothing more. I made the right decision because when I think about my future, I do not picture him with me.

I am still searching for the balance of my personal true happiness and that of others around me, for only here lies my self-contentment. I realize that I am a strong, independent young woman. I want to make decisions based upon what I want, and not how others want me to be. I know he wants me to be with him, but I cannot. This is the only time in my life when I can completely focus on myself. Lately I have noticed that my actions flow from my deepest, passionate longings. My personal drive comes from my own knowledge that I have the capacity to do wonderful things in my life.

It would have been extremely easy to reconcile with my former boyfriend and be happy for the moment, but I would rather have moments of sadness right now, and be secure in the decision that I have made. I have learned a multitude of things this year. I have discovered that I have an extraordinary passion for life, and I must take advantage of the constant influx of opportunities that come my way. I realize the importance of self-sufficiency, and how that is the key to happiness. I yearn for great successes in my professional life. Success will always be important to me. However, I do predict that I will encounter conflict between my personal and professional life, and I know at some point in time, I must decide what is more important to me: leaving my mark on the world, or investing myself in my husband and children wholeheartedly. (I am a traditional young woman insofar as I do want a family.) I also crave public recognition and have set remarkable goals for myself. I am willing to invest the requisite time on my journey to success.

I have confronted my anxieties about failed relationships, both currently in repair, with my father and my former boyfriend. If I repair my relationship with my father, I will have an easier time relating to the opposite sex. Moreover, if this bond is stable and secure, I do not risk a tainted, compensatory desire to find a man to love me. I know my father loves me, and he is remorseful for his atrocious actions. It has been difficult to accept the fact that I associate so closely with someone who subscribes to a different moral code than I; however, I forgive him and do not judge him any longer. Recently, I received an e-mail from my father's mistress. I did not share this with my mother, because I want to protect her from more pain, depression, and sorrow. My father's mistress apologized to me for being involved with my father, and for causing so much pain in my family. I never replied to the letter, mainly because I did not want to provide her with the satisfaction that I made any sort of time for her. However, I did not judge her, or her statements; I forgave and sympathized with her. My father fulfilled a part of her life that made her content for a certain time. Admittedly, this came at an enormous price—my mother's love for him has taken various different forms in the past year. I have learned that people fulfill themselves in different ways, obviously some more destructive and damaging than others. I believe that everyone has a void and tries to find different ways to fill his or her particular gap.

My former boyfriend and I are now close friends. As difficult as that position is for me to take, I take it with a great sense of relief and excitement. Now my self-exploration begins. I wish only good things for him as well. This course has taught me to look within myself and find my core. I often ask myself, what is the essence of Maria Santos? Who is she, and who does she aspire to be? I am a sensitive, emotional person who guards these two qualities with skepticism and realism. I expressed an enormous fear of shutting people out of my life simply because I am on a path of exploration. I fear people hurting me, and so I never completely let them in. However, I realize that by creating a machine of pre-programmed responses, I am not developing a soul. This is *not* the emotional investment—or divestment—I am willing to make for myself in the future. If I fail to develop my soul I will never possess the depth of character I wish to achieve. I also will not feel things as deeply as I intend to. I know I have made the right decisions after making them because I feel secure in my ability to evaluate my sentiments and positions regarding various circumstances.

I admire my former boyfriend's grace, and I admire his courage and capacity to be authentic in his acceptance of my need for individual liberty. Many times being truly authentic is frowned upon by society, as it is incongruous with social expectations. Many people advised him to shun me, but I am forever grateful that he took a different path, the path of forgiveness and understanding.

Maintaining a balance with regard to "sense and sensibility" is something I strive for. I am developing a natural cognitive understanding, especially in practical matters. At the same time, I never want to lose my ability to feel or to perceive. To be dulled of all emotional responses would diminish the meaning of my future relationships and successes. I hope to refine my awareness in matters of feeling. Throughout *Questions of Civilization*, Aristotle's notion that all knowledge comes from experience has served as my guide. He also emphasizes moderation as the key to moral virtue, and I believe this is what I am searching for. Often times, I lead my life with either much excess or deficiency. I believe that the quality of my life will improve, if I take the time to mend myself and embrace moderation. After I read *Genesis* this year, I found a quote I subscribe to in the *Old Testament*, *Ecclesiastes*, III, 1-3. "To every thing there is a season, and a time to every purpose under the heaven: A time to be born, and a time to die; a time to plant, and a time to pluck up that which is planted." My life is simply a series of graduations, from one place to the next, in which I will create and destroy things. Some relationships will live, and some will die. The colors of my life are constantly changing, and I look back on this year with much gratitude and the realization that this chapter of college life will inevitably close as well. So for now, I shall embrace the changing colors for as long as I can.

FREEDOM AND ORDER

Kyle Ragins

EVERY SOCIETY FACES A fundamental reciprocity between freedom and order. The more freedom a society grants its citizens, the less order exists; the more order present in a society, the less freedom its citizens have. This basic tradeoff is the essential dilemma of civilization. Both freedom and order have advantages, so the question arises: which is more important to create a successful society? The clear answer is that a society must reach an Aristotelian mean between the two extremes to create the ideal living environment.

In *The Analects*, Confucius presents the case for a society founded predominantly on order. In Book 12, Chapter 1, *The Analects* say, "Do not look at what is contrary to ritual, do not listen to what is contrary to ritual, and make no movement which is contrary to ritual." "Ritual" here is a translation of the Chinese word *li*, which encompasses not just rituals but all forms of convention, tradition, manners, and propriety. *Li* is the driving force that brings order to society. Confucius believes that no action that is not in strict accordance with the rituals, tradition, and order of established society can be good. In Book 1, Chapter 12, Confucius states that, "If you behave harmoniously because you understand harmony, but do not regulate your conduct with ritual, surely that cannot be made to work." Confucius seems to believe that a utopian society has no real need for freedom at all. If everyone were to act in accordance with tradition, people would achieve Confucius's ideal society.

Confucius's utopia is fundamentally flawed in its lack of freedom, because without freedom, progress, innovation, and creativity disappear. Western Civilization, and Americans in particular, are repulsed by the idea of a society where everyone acts in accordance with tradition, never challenging what came before them, and always preserving order. The reason for this is that Western Civilization values progress highly.

In his teachings, Confucius makes an implicit assertion that progress has no value by claiming that people should always conform to past ritual in their actions, rather than look to reform or progress. The idea that progress has no value is ludicrous. Although progress may not have nearly the importance Western Civilization places on it, there are certainly cases in which progress has had undeniable value. Progress eliminated the moral atrocities of slavery and human sacrifice. Progress led to scientific discoveries that have improved medical care, allowing people to live longer lives. Progress allowed for the diverse proliferation of all the types and genres of artwork that have touched the world.

Confucius seems to believe that the only thing that has value in the world is the order derived both from tradition and the wisdom of our ancestors. Yet if we analyze the effects that progress has had over the thousands of years of human civilization, even with respect to this emphasis on order, certain kinds of progress, too, have value. For example, improved medical care clearly increases the order in society; however, under Confucius's teachings, this sort of advance would be difficult or impossible. A scientist would only work within established theories and repeat past experiments, and thus remain likely only to reaffirm prior conclusions, because Confucius would not have the scientist break with tradition. People simply cannot realize the benefits of progress conforming with Confucius's ideal of acting only in accordance with what has been done before: never challenging *li*, but always letting it regulate and confine their conduct.

Not only is Confucius wrong about how people should behave to create the perfect society, he is also wrong about order being the only thing that has value in the world. There is another kind of value: an aesthetic value that exists in art. Confucius's teachings would only allow traditional Chinese artwork to exist in the world. Artists would be unable to innovate or create new methods and means of expressing their ideas, because they would be bound to regulate their conduct with *li*. Although traditional Chinese artwork has an aesthetic value, it can only go so far in expressing the myriad of emotions, ideas, and feelings that the people of the world strive to convey through artwork. Artistic progression achieves a much greater aesthetic value by allowing artists to try new and different things, breaking with *li*.

Just as the ideal society of Confucius may be flawed for lack of progress, a completely free society in which progress may abound also has its flaws. If people discard all traditions and are granted many freedoms, they may well be able to achieve progress by constantly trying new things, but at the expense of order—which clearly has its own value, even for progress. When people abandon tradition and order, chaos ensues. In such a society, there would be no means of predicting a person's actions based on standards of propriety, because he or she would be free to violate these standards at will. To echo Hobbes, people would, as a result, be unable to accomplish any large-scale goals; no one could be trusted to engage in contracts to cooperate towards a goal. Even more dangerous than this loss of cooperation is the violence and crime that would ensue on a mass scale when people have the freedom and inclination spontaneously to defy the traditional norms of conduct. This is exactly what one sees in riots. So clearly a completely free society is not a utopian one either.

If a completely free society is not ideal, and a society of perfect order is not ideal, it becomes evident that the ideal society must lie somewhere between the two. Up until this point, I have only dealt with extremes of freedom and order, but if I move away from these two extremes toward a balance between the two, many advantages start to appear. For example, a scientist who follows the tradition of the scientific method but at the same time is given the freedom to break away from traditional worldviews and methods of earlier scientists will be able to accomplish things of great value. This scientist is balancing the order of the scientific community with the freedom to move in new directions in order to achieve an ideal result. In the same way, societies should strive to achieve the perfect balance between freedom and order, to achieve ideal results.

Aristotle believed that morally virtuous actions were those that were a mean between two extremes. Although Aristotle meant his theory of moral virtue to apply primarily to personal actions, it seems that it can also be accurately applied to whole societies. Just as a person can achieve moral virtue by taking a mean path between two extremes, societies are most effective when they seek to achieve a balance between the two extremes of freedom and order. The history of human societies and the quest for a utopia is actually the story of the quest to reach equilibrium between freedom and order. The United States has come close to achieving this balance, but it is clear that the many freedoms this country has given its citizens have had less than an ideal effect. While these freedoms have led to rapid progress in all fields, the United States has also faced the breakdown of morals and increased crime rates. These problems make it clear that the United States is not a utopian society. We have not yet achieved the ideal balance between freedom and order. There is still work to be done, and we can only hope that someday, somewhere, a society will strike this perfect balance.

WOULD SOCRATES GET ACUPUNCTURE?

Carsten Belanich

....

"I would like to beg you, dear Sir, as well as I can, to have patience with every-thing unresolved in your heart and try to love the questions themselves as if they were locked rooms or books written in a very foreign language. Don't search for the answers, which could not be given to you now, because you would not be able to live them. And the point is, to live everything. Live the questions now. Perhaps then, someday far in the future, you will gradually, without even noticing it, live your way to the answer... those tasks that have been entrusted to us are difficult; almost everything serious is difficult; and everything is serious."

—Rainer Maria Rilke, from *Letters to a Young Poet*

EVEN BEFORE I WALKED in the door, the clinic looked a bit dodgy. The gold letters of "Claremont Acupuncture" were peeling off their plywood backing, which was itself mounted at a funny angle. Inside, the waiting room smelled strongly of what I sup-pose were medicinal herbs (and burnt offer-ings?). As for the needles, they seemed sterile enough as various parts of my body were per-forated by them, all while the "doctor" mused about my *qi* being severely out of whack. Laying there, in the half darkness, aware of the bizarre sensation of having electric current passed through subcutaneous pins in my scalp, calves, temples and thumbs, I could almost hear the strictly rational part of my brain screaming at me: *What are you doing, Carsten? This is contrary to everything you've ever learned since sixth grade about science! It's exactly the kind of dangerous, irrational quackery you rail against practically every day! It's veritably pre-Copernican!* Indeed, scheduling an appointment at an acupuncture clinic to treat my aching, foggy head was to a degree a reaction to all the real doctors who'd told me there was nothing I could do but wait it out, which for me implied going insane in the meantime. We do bizarre things when we are desperate. And by bizarre I mean irrational, because today what we cannot explain through established patterns of reason we call bizarre, strange and quackery. My first impulse would be to say "rightly so," for Science and Reason have changed humanity indisputably for the better over the past five hundred years. (Thank God we don't *only* have acupuncture to treat post-concussion syndrome!) But the very fact that both Claremont Acupuncture Clinic, trailing clouds of herb-smoke, and Pomona Valley Medical Center, with its X-rays, MRIs and sterile surgery, exist a few miles away from each other—and both stay in business—means that this fight between Reason and Romanticism has not been truly resolved, either at the societal or the personal level.

Thus we moderns are faced with a constant question which ultimately we must answer for ourselves: Where do we draw the line in our lives between Reason and Romanticism, Science and Mysticism, Rationality and Faith? In other words, how should we view and explain the world? Clearly, the choice is not, in reality, strictly between one category or the other, for even we, the partisans of the Enlightenment, go to acupuncture clinics, and even the "doctor" leaning over me a few days ago explained his technique using a strange mix of traditional Chinese medical terms and neurophysiology. We are decidedly undecided about where to draw this line, and to our detriment. For myself, I want at the very least to have guidelines of where and how to draw this theoretical line that are as clear as possible: Socrates' admonition about that distinct pitfall of an "unexamined life" seems enough reason to me as to why I would want such a thing, and vacillating without thought between Pomona Valley and Claremont Acupuncture sure doesn't seem like living up to his standard. Even more broadly, though, is that if we all, in some ideal future, could strike a thought-through balance between Reason and Romanticism in our own lives and articulate our reasoning, then as a whole society we might just arrive at a point where we could extract the best out of both: MDs, for example, might not feel such a need to blindly assault the "quacks," and the acupuncturists, osteopaths and cranio-sacral practitioners might stop railing against Western medicine's myopic focus on the symptoms (and not the roots) of medical problems. I anxiously await the day when we know everything scientifically, but until then we might as well acknowledge that science and rationality don't have a complete monopoly on truth quite yet and—in the spirit of Odysseus and Aristotle—get down to the business of how we should actually lead our lives in a world that is both rational and mysterious.

I've had the taste of this question in my mouth for some time now, but it's so big and fundamental that often it's hard to tell that there's even a real question to be faced. Every now and then it's been dragged to the surface, though, by books like Robert Pirsig's *Zen and the Art of Motorcycle Maintenance,* a classic meditation on the nature of what the author calls the "romantic" and "classical" worldviews carried on through a motorcycle trip across my beloved Pacific Northwest. Above all, Pirsig points out that neither outlook by itself is fully adequate to describe the world we live in. Previously, as I've said, I wasn't even really aware that there was much of a divide! I had, though, in a way already learned some *of Motorcycle Maintenance's* lesson on my own: There was a time in my life when I had been passionately religious and loathed the whole modern way of seeing the world, a result of getting fed up with what I had considered the arrogance of science—I wanted to live on faith and emotion alone. Ultimately, however, I found this unsatisfying (for reasons which became clear only later) and for a while drifted to the polar opposite, a kind of cynical resentment of faith and religion and a complete devotion to science and rationality and secularism. It's easy to see how both of these positions are somewhat distant from the Aristotelian-Odyssean mean. To move forward, I had to acknowledge that both extreme Romanticism and Reason bred the kind of unsavory orthodoxy I wanted to avoid; as I've already said, I've realized that the question of where to draw the line between those two is so complicated and personal that striking a compromise is implied.

Gradually, I've found the vocabulary needed to think about this whole problem in a serious way. Descartes' dualism, essentially a way of responding to my question, seemed for a long time the most pleasant way of reconciling the two, with the *res cogitans* (mind) standing in for the romantic element and the *res extensa* (body) for the rational one. Deal with them separately and everything will work out. (Not to mention that the Counter-Reformation Church may stop breathing down your neck!). Ultimately, though, I came to believe that this is simply to sidestep the question, and while Descartes' idea shows a way in which the two worldviews could possibly exist simultaneously within us, in my opinion it does not function well as a practical guide. If anything, Descartes' attempts to prove the existence of God in a quasi-scientific way reveal a personality still slightly uncomfortable with the co-existence of Romanticism and Classicism as a viable way of seeing the world. Thus I had to turn somewhere else in order to move towards a satisfactory resolution.

To start, I can define what I see as the extremes. On the one hand, Freud, among others, gives us an example of how to take the rational too far: Doing so, art becomes a "narcotic," and religion becomes simply a "palliative measure," shielding us from a life which clearly "is too hard for us." (*Civilization and Its Discontents*) In all honesty, I will admit that this may even be true in a purely rational sense. But, the first of my objections is that Freud's point presents a problem without a real solution. He gives us facts that in the end don't change much for us as we actually live our lives, just as if the Grand Unified Theory were discovered tomorrow, we would all be impressed, but human life would just keep going on, no more or less mysterious, daunting and beautiful than before. On the other hand, letting oneself be overwhelmed by the mystery of the world and surrendering completely to the romantic view—and then often to the guidance of faith and tradition by joining a mendicant order, etc.—is an equally grave mistake. Just as Freud can make one wonder why we should keep on living in the first place, *The Nun's Story* made me wonder why one would want to spend his or her entire life solely preparing for death. I've been to these poles before, and, again, neither is appealing to me. So where does my ideal middle ground lie?

Predictably, it is with the Greeks, bless them. And perhaps a Russian, too, for, as Charles Guignon points out in his introduction to *The Brothers Karamazov*, it is Dostoevsky who argues most persuasively that the true value of a worldview is not its abstract truth but its *viability,* its ability to guide us to the fullest experience of human life. To me, neither the world-view of Freud nor that of the Benedictines produce ideal ways of living in the here-and-now, but perhaps Dostoevsky's Christ does, asserting in response to Freud's proxy, the Grand Inquisitor, that "Man does not live by bread alone," while simultaneously rejecting the "miracle, mystery and authority" which the Mother Superior tries so hard to foist upon poor Sister Luke in *The Nun's Story*. That said, it is Socrates who now comes first in my mind as a model of rationality tempered by humility and even a hint of faith: For him, reason leads not only to a set of livable moral precepts, but the realization that our own knowledge of the universe is tiny and that we must therefore proceed carefully and with humility—"that whatever I do not know, I do not even suppose I know." (*The Apology of Socrates*) This is clearly that crucial acknowledgement of the current limits of human knowledge which I find often lacking on the extreme end of the "rational" worldview. Coming from the wisest man in all of Athens, such an admonition is to be heeded. Socrates' speculation about the nature of death in the *Apologia* is in much the same spirit—rationally thought out, but acknowledging knowledge's limits and ultimately hopeful. What's more, while he rejects the dogma of the religion of the Athenian state, he still refers often to "gods," if not necessarily personified ones, then at the very least those which represent the mysterious—but ultimately understandable—forces of Nature. (It is also interesting to note that when facing his death in *Phaedo*, Socrates begins composing poetry, reversing his long-standing criticism of artists.) Clearly, even the great tactician of argument himself recognized the potential value of the romantic element of human existence.

Considering Dostoevsky's Christ and Socrates side by side, a certain moderate ideal begins to emerge: A worldview based fundamentally in reason which acknowledges its own intrinsic limits, leaving room at its fringes for a kind of rational faith. This faith is strong precisely because it has been arrived at by the individual using his or her great natural gift of reason, and precisely by virtue of this rationality, it is also self-limiting, not prone to dogmatism. Admittedly, I'm not quite sure if either of my role models would actually frequent the Claremont Acupuncture Clinic, but at the very least their combined example sets up a framework for evaluating whether or not I should do so, which would go something like this: "There is little scientific basis for acupuncture's efficacy, but having done my research, it also presents little danger to my health, insurance will cover the cost, and there is plenty of anecdotal evidence that it does indeed work for some unknown reason. Thus, I will at least try it because I have nothing to lose other than an hour from my day—and that loud-mouthed, extremist, strictly rational part of my brain be damned!" With this in mind, I went back to that hazy waiting room this morning and again had my *qi* ostensibly realigned. For whatever reason, I've felt great all day.

Acupuncture is, however, only one of those small yet crucial dilemmas we face daily in which Romanticism is pitted against Rationality. In the end, we must confront these dilemmas on our own, however scary that may be. Certainly, it is comforting to know that others have chosen consistently and well between those two poles, but even with their solid framework for doing so in hand, every day seems a challenge, and—even worse—an invitation to let someone else do your thinking for you, or just to drop such considerations altogether. May I never give in to such an impulse.

BODY AND SOUL

Jordan C. Stewart

SOMETIMES, WHEN I WRITE my name on a piece of paper I take a moment and just stare at the word Jordan. I think "Jordan... Jordan... Jordan" with different intonations, realizing that "Jordan" is more than just a word, or a name; rather, it is who I am—my identity. Amidst the stare and the deep thoughts, my bones quiver and my heart jumps, causing a weird, indescribable feeling throughout my body. This feeling reminds me that I, Jordan Stewart, am a living human being, with a body, an identity and a purpose. This is puzzling to me. Who chose me to be here? Why do I have a beating heart and a pensive brain? What does it really mean to be Jordan Stewart? These questions amount to the conflict that plagues everyone's hearts and minds: "What does it mean to be human?" When I experience this indescribable emotion while thinking deeply of my name, I believe that my soul and my body connect in a way that reminds me that I am human. I believe that I am human because my experiences, thoughts, emotions and soul connect on a level greater than both religion and science can explain. Though this is what I believe, I do not know for sure, and will never know for sure, and this ineffable uncertainty itself encompasses much of what it means to be human—that unremitting drive to search for truth in one's own life.

As a part of life, we have both controllable and uncontrollable experiences. The nature of my experiences does not matter. What matters is how the experiences affect me as a person. I believe that part of being human is taking my experiences, recognizing them as truths in my own life, and allowing them to imprint my soul, which therefore enhances my thoughts and my emotions. For example, through experience, I have concluded that it is good to be an honest, happy and a "Marianne-like" person, whereas others might see otherwise. Thoughts and emotions, in my opinion, come from something more than just neurons firing in the brain. This materialist view rejects the idea of a soul, in which I firmly believe. Though my basis for this belief is still obscure, souls, to me, are a part of all human beings. Perhaps, it is a soul that defines being human. However, there are many religious and sacrilegious challenges to this belief that cause me to continue to search for what it means to be human beyond having a soul.

Religion and God together constitute an aspect of life that I have begun to question in terms of their connections with being human. As I stated in a previous paper, God connects with my soul and therefore God connects with me. However, as I have thought more deeply about being human as it relates to religion, I have become skeptical.

Presently, a large body of evidence in science and society rejects both God and the Bible. For example, in the Bible, God condemns homosexuals, and this causes me to ask whether such behavior is a complex choice with moral implications or simply a manifestation of our genetic make-up. Although there is no definitive evidence on whether homosexuality is indeed something chosen or something given, I personally cannot fathom how it could ever be a choice. Thus the possibility that people are genetically predisposed to be homosexual is, to me, the more plausible. If God condemns homosexuality, then the link—at least for me—between God and His creation becomes obscure. If God is indeed the designer and creator of mankind, then would He not be a hypocrite for condemning homosexuals while allowing them to be born?

I have raised the matter of homosexuality because it is an issue close to home: my brother is gay. I love my brother and accept his ways; however, according to the Bible, God does not. This then conflicts with my own views in regard to believing in the word of God, but also loving and accepting my brother for who he is. I know that my brother is human, which further muddles my view that being human and God are connected. What I have come to believe, then, from the evidence presented thus far, is that religion does not necessarily define the human being or humanity. This is a regrettable conclusion for me because it is incompatible with what my religion has taught me: that God is indeed the creator of all humans.

I could assume a similar standpoint to René Descartes in *Discourse on Method*. Though his celebrated method led him to reject or to doubt conventional truths, he contended that there is a God, who in turn resolves most of our doubts. Up until this point in my life, I never really questioned the existence of God and, like Descartes, used God to resolve my own doubts about the world. When questioning why I am a human on this earth, I held to the belief that it was God's will for me to be the daughter of my mother and father. However, now that I reevaluate the ills of society and the discontinuities between the Bible and today's societal and scientific realities, Descartes' style of relentless self-interrogation seems more and more appropriate. As I have stated before, I am a Christian and I do believe in God: but neither have I ever felt the real presence of God in my life, nor have I ever participated in my own search for God. Both this direct sense of otherness and the search yet await me. Still, I believe that it will not hurt to believe in God, even though His very existence remains unknown. Even if there is no proof that God exists, I would rather be safe in believing in God and that Jesus Christ died for our sins, than possibly be sorry after death.

To further investigate the question, "What does it mean to be human?", I have considered the case of animals. I mentioned in a previous paper that animals have experiences, feel emotions and are able think; therefore, they, too, have souls. If this is the case, I cannot use the soul to define the human being. Likewise, if one defines humans by their divine origins, then to the extent that God is held to have created animals, too, why do we not consider animals to be human? Implicitly—though humankind is unlikely to admit as much—we define ourselves as humans based on our appearance and our ability to be civilized. Animals may think, feel and experience as humans do, but they do not look or act like us, and therefore we do not consider them human.

The novel *You Shall Know Them*, by Vercors, to a certain extent confirms this idea. One of the arguments raised in connection with the humanity of the *tropis* asserts, "Mankind resembles a very exclusive club. What we call human is defined by us alone. The rules within the club are valid for us alone, and hence the need for a legal basis to be established, as much for the admission of new members as for setting up rules and regulations applicable to all." (240) With regard to our feelings and emotions versus those of animals, we hear, "...I wouldn't for an empire change that pain or even that horror, and even our lies and selfishness and hate, for their unconsciousness, for their happiness." (244) To me, this distinctly shows that the definition of a human goes beyond feelings and emotions into something exclusive to humankind. I do not know what that extra something is. Perhaps, it is right in front of our noses and is nothing more than that we, of all living things, have developed ourselves to be something greater in this world—perhaps we simply lie at the apex of fitness in the sense intended by Charles Darwin. Whatever the case, we are indeed "a very exclusive club."

Having just mentioned Darwin, I must admit that I have an issue with science trying to define what it means to be human. Science is beginning to make humanity seem very systematic and objective. This belief leaves little room for the root of emotion and passion in a human's life, which I believe is one of the most important parts of being human. This, of course, relates to my belief that souls carry the emotion, the passion and the thoughts derived from experience. If science continues to carry the entire burden of definition, we could turn into the society that Richard Rorty describes in "Persons without Minds," focusing on the "C-fibers" and state of the "S-296." This unfortunate possibility could result in humanity losing sight of the emotions and true feelings that are embedded in our souls and remind us that we are alive.

Along the same lines, I know that a machine will never be able to compare to a human, even if the genius Alan Turing argues otherwise in his famous essay, "Computing Machinery and Intelligence." A machine is completely explainable down to its finest wire. Humans, on the other hand, are not, and will never be. Though scientists and engineers may create a subassembly in a machine that can *act* as a soul, the true soul is different: machines passively experience the world—if at all!—by being programmed; humans actively experience by living.

Understandably so, we reached no conclusion in class when trying to define humanity, thus proving Vercors's quote: "The mere existence of disagreement is the first proof that, on the one hand, ultimate truth is denied us—else how could we disagree?—and on the other, that we go on seeking it—else why argue about it?" (246) I believe that one may try to define being human, but always finds a flaw in the definition flowing from some indelible discontinuity between humanity and everything else. I believe that there is something to being human beyond what science and religion can explain in something that I call a soul, an entity that does not necessarily implicate religion. I believe that humans possess something intangible and soul-like, imprinted by experiences but yielding no objectifiable characterization. The human condition of searching for this intangible, soul-like entity might be summed up by Gotthold Efraim Lessing's statement: "Not the truth in whose possession some human being is or thinks he is, but the honest trouble he has taken to get behind the truth is what constitutes the worth of a human being.... If God held in his closed right hand all the truth and in his left hand only the ever live drive for truth, albeit with the addition that I should always and evermore err, and he said to me: Choose! I should humbly grab his left hand, saying: Father, give! Pure truth is after all for you alone!" I too, would "humbly grab His left hand." Until God proves Himself concrete, human or animal souls become tangible, or science proves God and religion fallacious, the question "what does it mean to be human?" will never be answered, but will always be actively searched.

I accept that this question is unanswerable, and I accept that I have beliefs, such as my belief in God and souls, that do not have any legitimate proof. This, I believe, is part of being human and the purpose of life—to search for nonexistent answers. It is not just the question of being human that is unanswerable. Questions of morality, God, and art do not have universal answers, but they do have a unique, indefinite, exploratory value and essence for each of us. This is because the will for a human to search for one's own answers to these questions is the reason why one is alive. As summed up beautifully by Socrates, "The unexamined life is not worth living." Thus, I continue to examine, continue to experience, and continue to live, recognizing only one truth, which occurs with a shivering of my bones as I simply just stare at my name.

BELOVED

....

Athena Cabot

ACTION ON BEHALF OF love can sometimes surface in forms unrecognizable to the public eye. In Toni Morrison's novel, *Beloved*, the guilty mother, Sethe, exemplifies this idea when she murders her infant daughter, and attempts to kill her other three children, to save them from being forced into a life of slavery. Sethe is surrounded by a society that shuns her crime mostly because it fails to understand the psychology behind her deed. By examining Sethe's demoralizing experiences from Sweet Home, her brutal crime becomes understandable. Sethe finds it unbearable that her world is controlled by white men, and by attempting to take the lives of her children she attempts to rid them of this painful reality. I believe that Sethe's actions are justifiable because they are carried out with the intention of protecting those that she loves. Society is held accountable for her murderous decision because it accepts the horrific institution of slavery without sympathizing with its victims. Both Sethe's justified actions and society's responsibility for these actions amount to evidence supporting the truth behind the idea that an individual's circumstances do justify their behavior, even when it is extreme.

Via Sethe's traumatic recollections of her past, it is clear that her incentive in killing Beloved is purely driven by her desire to shelter her family from the abusive control of others. During her time in Sweet Home, Sethe is reduced to something less than human as she is physically violated. When the schoolteacher's nephews steal Sethe's milk, she experiences an ultimate sense of objectification in which she is not a human being, but something less: an animal, a milked cow. This impacts Sethe greatly, as she feels just as demoralized as if she had been raped—she is stripped of her power to protect herself and is forced to surrender her milk, milk that Nature intended for *her* baby. Sethe's resentment of the sexual assault is reinforced by her mother's history of being raped. Sethe's mother took pride in Sethe because she was the only child born from consensual sex. The knowledge of her mother's history of being physically mistreated and her own experience with physical violation heavily contributes to Sethe's need to kill her children. When schoolteacher comes to re-enslave Sethe and her children, Sethe is desperate to break the vicious cycle and prevent her children from potentially enduring the physical abuse that she did.

Sethe's actions are further justified by the degrading emotional situations that she encountered in Sweet Home. Sethe remembers schoolteacher cruelly instructing his students to list both the human and the animal characteristics describing her features. Consequently, Sethe is rudely awakened to the dehumanizing lessons of the schoolteacher, who instills ideas regarding her supposed inferiority in the minds of others. Thus, it is with good reason that Sethe strives to save her children—by taking their lives she will exempt them from knowing the ugliness of the life she has seen. Stamp Paid supports this when he says, "She ain't crazy. She loved those children. She was trying to out-hurt the hurter." I believe that Sethe's sole purpose in attempting to kill her children is to undermine evil men like schoolteacher from affecting her loved ones.

Society is responsible for Sethe's difficult decision because it chooses to live with the injustices of slavery, yet doesn't tolerate the people who act out against these injustices. By watching the demoralization of people and not acting against it, society forces individuals like Sethe to struggle for their own liberation and for that of those they love. By being passive, society forces people to resort to desperate measures in order to accomplish something or to prove a point. Those around Sethe submit to injustice by accepting that they are considered inferior. In a scene with Sixo, Morrison shows the supposed elevated status of whites: "Clever, but schoolteacher beat him anyway to show him that definitions belonged to the definers— not the defined." I think this expression can be appropriately attributed to Sethe's fear that her children will be "defined." Sethe doesn't want her children to live a subordinate life where someone like schoolteacher can dictate the way they will live. Morrison describes Baby Suggs' hardship with losing children: "Sixty years of losing children to the people who chewed up her life and spit it out like a fish bone." Those around Sethe yield to the injustices of everyday practices in Sweet Home by allowing their families to be bought and used. Sethe, on the other hand, realizes that if she takes the life of her own children she thwarts the power of those who do not deserve it. She thinks that it is better that she, who loves her children, decides their fate. By witnessing the weak attempts of those around her to overcome the miseries of slave life, Sethe is forced to break free of society's norm and make her monumental choice.

An individual's circumstances do justify behavior that would traditionally be considered unacceptable. I believe that individuals can act outrageously in reaction to the injustices of their environment in order to make a change. These individuals are misunderstood because others are unable to see the true motives behind their criminal acts. In *Beloved*, when Sethe first goes to Cincinnati, she discovers the bliss of freedom, and she becomes aware of the stark difference between the oppressiveness of Sweet Home and the liberating beauty of a free life. Thus Sethe finds it hard to let her children be forced into a cruel life of slavery knowing that there are much better things, like freedom, out there. Baby Suggs describes what freedom feels like: "These hands belong to me. These my hands," and we hear in the narration that follows, "[S]he felt a knocking in her chest and discovered something else new: her own heartbeat." I think this is precisely the exhilaration that Sethe feels when she realizes the wonders of freedom—I think Sethe believes living within the bounds of slavery and not having "your own hands" or "your own heartbeat" is not living at all. Thus while her actions toward her children seem violent, they are meant to save her children from being confined to a hateful, pre-determined life. Sethe loves her children too much to let them be deprived of something as valuable and necessary as freedom, and in this I strongly agree that conventionally intolerable behavior can sometimes be justified by individual circumstances.

While Sethe's actions seem unforgivably severe, they are justifiable considering the circumstances in which she struggles and society's passiveness in attacking the ills which Sethe witnesses in the world. Ultimately, it is Sethe's immense love for her children that drives her to such great heights to protect them. She tells Paul D, "Love is or it ain't. Thin love ain't love at all." It is from Sethe's unconditional love that her great sacrifice is born.

The Nature and Impact of Art

Janice Claire Serrano Tan

I HAVE TAKEN ART courses for most of my life, and have gone through many phases as an artist. In preschool, I would knit my brows in concentration while coloring, fiercely willing my chubby fingers to color within the solid black lines of the coloring book. In middle school, I explored various mediums and techniques, and discovered that I favored sculpting and painting. In my freshman year of high school, I strove to perfect my sculpting and painting skills, focusing entirely upon the appearance of my work with no regard whatsoever for its actual significance. However, when I began the International Baccalaureate Art course in tenth grade, a class which I would continue to take over the next three years, my whole perspective on art changed dramatically. IB Art is a course designed to give aspiring artists a better understanding of the purpose of art, as well as what differentiates a pretty picture from artwork. And yet after the first few months of the course, I was more than ready to give up on art.

Unlike previous art courses, IB Art judged my work based not only upon its aesthetic appearance, but also on its significance and depth. My fellow art students and I were encouraged (and sometimes even required) to incorporate culture into our artwork, specifically our own cultures. At first, I loathed this class because I felt as if my creativity was being beaten into submission by an emotionless, rigid grading criterion. My first few pieces were terrible, lacking in inspiration, unmotivated and downright rubbish. For months I struggled with finding even a glimmer of an idea that would hopefully lead me towards my next painting. I was angry at myself and frustrated with art. I both looked forward to and dreaded every art class: looked forward because of that growing feeling of excitement I got whenever I gazed upon the freshly gessoed white expanse of a blank canvas and considered its infinite potential, and dreaded for fear of being unable to realize even a fraction of that potential.

However, right when I was just about ready to quit art, my sketchbook research ventured into a topic close to my heart: *family*. I was half-heartedly viewing the gradual empowerment of women throughout Chinese history—a very interesting topic but one that I would discuss with an aloof sort of scholarly detachment—when I chanced upon two events that would propel me into a whirlwind of ideas and entrench me in my artwork. First was a trip to China with my parents, brother and Chinese grandmother, and the next was a conversation with a Chinese friend about her father.

I have always loved my family, and to a certain extent I have always been aware of the intensity of my devotion to them, but sometimes I would still be embarrassed by some of the things my parents do, such as my Dad's habit of speaking while chewing his food and the way my Mom would put her hair up in slightly crooked ponytails. However, unlike my parents' embarrassing little quirks, my grandmother's conventional Chinese behavior afforded me complete and utter mortification. Chinese mannerisms are vastly different from western ones, and through western eyes, they may seem very crude. My grandmother would sometimes burp in public, thinking it was perfectly acceptable to do so, slurp her soup and stuff cookies into her bag at buffets. Up until my sophomore year I had never been able to understand these seemingly crude mannerisms and would oftentimes be embarrassed to be out in public with my grandmother, no matter how much I loved her.

Yet being in China with my family and grandmother was like stepping into another world. I was surprised at the clarity with which I began to understand Chinese culture. The many values of filial piety, respect for the elderly, etc., were values that I realized I understood and have even adopted as my own. I am not saying that the Chinese culture is perfect, and in many ways it can drive me completely insane with its rigid, almost foolish respect for elders and somewhat inferior view of women.

Being in China and experiencing their way of life made me realize how silly some of my western values were. Without having to worry about being embarrassed or frowned upon, I began to realize that my parents' and grandmother's quirks did not really matter to me at all! Who cares if my dad speaks with his mouth full? At least he doesn't just sit stoically at the dinner table, without even bothering to ask me about my day. And in fact, I would rather have a mother who cares more about testing out different cooking recipes and watching Korean dramas with me than fiddling with her hair and fussing about her appearance. Somehow adhering to western mannerisms just seemed so insignificant in the grand scheme of things. I would rather have my Dad chattering away about work, relatives and weekend plans, than to have perfect table manners, even if it would be looked down upon by our friends and acquaintances. It makes me happy to hear my Dad's voice, to speak to him and hear him asking me about my studies, opinions and frivolous little problems. It seems illogical to sacrifice happiness for maintaining a good image. I feel guilty whenever I think about how I was ashamed of my parents' little quirks, and this guilt is amplified greatly when I think of how unfair I was to my grandmother. Now that I think about it, my *Ama* (Chinese for "grandmother") doesn't even like cookies. That cookie that she packs away at buffets is the very same cookie that she gives me and my brother to share later on in the day.

The second significant event was a conversation with a really good Chinese friend of mine who was having problems with her father. She was angry that her father was pressuring her to excel in her studies and to get into a good college, which is common in Chinese families. She went on to complain about how her father forbade her from having a boyfriend, gave her a midnight curfew, and so on and so forth. However, the more I listened, the more I began to realize that the problem was not her father anymore: it was she. I am usually a very tolerant person, and it is very difficult to upset me. However, when it comes to self-pity and pessimism, I just explode.

In this case, I did not outwardly explode because I knew that it might do more harm than good. However, I just wanted to jump up, shake her and shout, "What's wrong with you?" I could not fathom why she did not notice that her father was only looking out for her wellbeing. My parents have even more strict rules for me, but in fact they have little application because I myself was never interested in activities that would involve said rules. I never went out to party late at night, preferring instead to play Monopoly with my brother until I drove him to bankruptcy at around one o'clock in the morning. (Of course, we kept our voices down and whispered taunts to each other so that Mom wouldn't force us to go to bed.) I've never had a boyfriend because I do not love easily and would often be brutally realistic about romance and relationships. As for studies, they have always come in at a distant second to my family, and my parents understand this. They insist that I do well in school because it is for my own future wellbeing, but they understand that studies should not compromise my health and happiness. I might seem to others as a dorky "goody-two-shoes," but partying, promiscuity and teenage freedoms have never appealed me.

Sometimes I feel out of place because of this, but I simply cannot force myself to go out, drink, party and stretch my non-existent curfew when I know that my brother is waiting at home for me with the monopoly board all set up on his bedroom floor. And how could I possibly go out on a date with a guy that I hardly even care about, when I know that I could instead be out watching a movie with my family, and afterwards waging a "discreet" food fight against my brother at some restaurant?

It seemed so wrong for my friend to condemn her father for expressing his concern for her. In fact, it didn't seem fair because when she explained to me exactly how he pressured her by scolding her and telling her his past hardships as a young man, it seemed much more benign than I'd originally thought based on her tears and passionate declarations of loathing. After she had finished explaining and I understood the situation more clearly, I was very rapidly losing patience with her and her continued ranting. I know it is customary for adolescents and even adults to complain and whine to their friends about their parents, and I can tolerate it when it is done in a joking manner. However, seriously complaining and condemning one's loved and loving ones for acting in her best interest is unbearable to me. I can tolerate laziness, stinginess, rudeness, and many other ill-behaviors—I'm guilty of some of them—but I cannot tolerate incessant, unjustified whining!

It seems illogical to whine about life when life is a blessing that must be lived to the fullest. No matter how bad one's life becomes, there is always some good in it, but that good can never be realized if one wallows in self-pity. If there's something you do not like about your life, then act upon it! In the case of my friend, I advised her to speak to her father and also to try to see things from his perspective. Again I suppressed my anger and frustration with her behavior, and my temptation to cry out, "Shut up and grow up!" I could not bear to see her misunderstand her father's concern, and mistake his love for spite. I was not really angry with her; I was just angry that she is missing the opportunity to love and appreciate her father, instead spending her time hating him and condemning him. I guess I just could not stand to see such an important thing as love be turned into hatred because of such foolish immaturity. Perhaps if her father had been truly an oppressive tyrant, then my opinion would have been vastly different, but to me he sounded like just another traditional Chinese father, striving to cope with his westernized teenage daughter's increasing demands for freedom. I sincerely hope that she realizes this and finds the same love for her parents as I have for mine.

So how did these experiences help me understand art? The tremendous significance of these events to me, as well as my immense emotional involvement with them made me realize that this is what artists paint, draw and sculpt. These are the things that songs are written for and movies are made of. True art is being able to capture one's own passionate beliefs and express them in a painting, a song, a play. Art is not about pretty pictures; art is about images and songs that convey the profound revelations of life that the artist happens to stumble upon. Aesthetics is only a part of what makes a good painting.

So why is it necessary for a work of art to demonstrate excellent artistic skill and striking aesthetics? If I were to bake my Mom a birthday cake, I would do my very best to make it as beautiful and tasty as possible. I would choose her favorite flavor, deplete my savings to buy the very best ingredients and decorations, and stir the cake batter until my arm falls off. It does not decrease the significance of my efforts and love for my Mom if the cake turns out to be the most atrocious culinary monstrosity the world has ever seen, but because I love my Mom, I would settle for no less than making the very best cake that I can. It is the same with artists. An issue that they feel strongly about must be painted as well as possible, not because aesthetics takes priority over meaning, but rather because the importance of the meaning deserves to be portrayed with the very best aesthetics. That is why I strive to make my paintings as aesthetically excellent as I possibly can.

I did not paint anything about my family or my friend's situation, simply because I could not even begin to fathom how I would go about fitting all my emotions onto a single canvas. I was also afraid that my limited art skills would not do justice to the depth of my emotions. For whatever reason, I never did manage to paint anything about my family. However, I now had a direction and a purpose to create art.

I began looking into the family values of various cultures, and was astonished by what I found out about the Filipinos. I met many low- to medium-income Filipinos on various community service trips, as well as those working on my school's janitorial faculty, and each and every time I realized one thing: Filipinos are very happy people. But why? I received many answers, ranging from the gardener's happiness that his plants were growing well, to a restaurant server's recent marriage. However, three reasons that each and every person gave were: God, hope and family. One of our school's gardeners, Bernard, has led a very difficult life. His father died when he was still in high school, so he was forced to quit school to find a job to support his mother and siblings. (I believe he had either eight or ten.) I was astonished at this discovery: Bernard always seemed so happy. He could often be found strolling down the hallways, swinging his watering can and wishing students a good day. The source of his happiness was that even though his life seemed difficult, he was actually very blessed because he had a loving family—his mother was still alive—and undiminishing hope for the future. Perhaps his siblings will finish college and become successful, or perhaps he will be promoted to head janitor someday.

I was very excited and pleased to have realized this about Bernard and many other low-income Filipinos because it was also what I believed. As a very stubborn, oftentimes bull-headed optimist, I always try to believe the very best in people and life. Hope is a must for me, and so is gratitude. Every day and even twice, thrice a day I thank God for my family and I thank my family for being so wonderful. I am even thankful that my brother is such an annoying little brat! Listening to the Filipinos that I have spoken to, as well as reflecting upon my own self, I have determined that the source of happiness is actually gratitude. When one is thankful, then one appreciates family, God and other blessings. It is the appreciation and awareness of how blessed we are that will bring people happiness, because it allows them to enjoy their family and their life.

However, I am not so completely naive that I believe that gratitude will fix all our problems. There is such a thing as suffering and it cannot be avoided or ignored, not even by an optimist. These low-income Filipinos that I have spoken to have very real, almost tangible happiness; however, their problems are just as real as their blessings, and their suffering is just as real as their happiness. In my painting (below) of one of my school's custodians, I tried to emphasize the conflicting emotions of Filipinos. On the one hand, they are very blessed with their families, etc. On the other hand, they also wish that they were in a better situation, and that their sufferings would disappear. In my painting, the custodian is gazing out into the school's courtyard, but it is difficult to say whether or not he is looking out in calm appreciation of the beauty of the school, blaming God for his current state of poverty, gazing in envy at the privileged lives of students and teachers, or maybe just reveling in the hope of a better future. I believe that he is doing all of these things because suffering can never be ignored, but the existence of suffering should never be a reason to forsake blessings and happiness.

If something were to happen to my loved ones, I could not even begin to describe how devastated I would be. I once met a fellow student whose father was telling me about how his brothers had died in the Vietnam War, and his son said logically and without hesitation that, "I would kill myself if Alan [his younger brother] died." That is exactly how I feel about my loved ones, but I know that it would also bring them immense grief if I were to kill myself on their account. My intense devotion to those I love is a difficult thing to handle. What does one do with such overwhelming emotions? How should I behave if that overwhelming love became overwhelming grief? It is a frightening thought, and one that I do not have an answer to. But one thing that I can say for sure, I have loved and have received love, and this experience can never be taken away from me. Perhaps it can be passed on to others.

Painting by Janice Tan. Reprinted with permission.

MARIANNE ON FREUD

Chelsea Norell

WHY DO WE CRAVE success? What is it that makes the satisfaction of success superior to any other joy in our lives? Why do we need another's approval to validate how we feel about ourselves? J.D. Salinger, quoting psychoanalyst Wilhelm Stekel writes, "The mark of the immature man is that he wants to die nobly for a cause, while the mark of the mature man is that he wants to live humbly for one." (*The Catcher in the Rye*) But do we ever achieve the "maturity" Salinger writes about? While the circumspect Odysseus seems to achieve Salinger's ideal, even he acquiesces to the flattery of the princess. Homer does not let him get away with it however; the results are fatal, as he almost loses sight of his mission. But is "living humbly" really our mission in life? Like Achilles, I would much rather live a shorter, exhilarating life and be remembered, than a long peaceful life and be forgotten. This could simply be the Marianne in me, but I would rather risk my emotional balance for extreme happiness than live complacently with no sense of extremity.

How could Achilles face the most harrowing villains on the face of the Earth without flinching, yet live with the unrelenting fear of dying without *kleos* (imperishable glory)? Salinger also writes, "I'm sick of not having the courage to be an absolute nobody." (*Franny and Zooey*) This quote resonates with me. What are Achilles and the rest of us afraid of? During a conversation between Achilles and Odysseus in the underworld, Achilles tells Odysseus that he wishes he were alive, on whatever modest terms, rather than having achieved *kleos* but now dead. I don't believe Achilles for a heartbeat. When I look back on high school, I always think that I wish I had taken more time to relax and hang out with my friends and not have worked so hard; however, I quickly realize that I could never have let myself work, study, or stress any less than I did, and furthermore, I wouldn't have been any happier if I had. It is easy to look at the ways you could have been happier in retrospect, but it is not only futile, it is unrealistic because there is no way of knowing the consequences of your hypothetical actions, and thus you have no way of gauging whether or not you would have been happier. It's pleasant to believe you have discovered where you went wrong and how to make yourself happier in the future, but for someone like me, slowing down is never really a viable option.

Maybe "success" is a Platonic conception; something tenuous that exists outside of us. Maybe it's never truly attainable, and we seek it because it is unconquerable. Akin to Freud's superego, we strive to satisfy it wholeheartedly, while secretly knowing that we will never attain it. Why is it human nature to set ourselves up for that kind of demise? Ivan Ilych must have known in the back of his mind that the treadmill he was on would ultimately leave him in the same place. He even knew that it would leave him without the joy that makes life tolerable. We all know this, and yet we don't step off.

Before I appear too critical of the treadmill cycle, I must qualify my statements. I know exactly why we don't step off. Our superegos, the Achilles inside each of us, convince us that we can defy the cycle, that for us personally, life is a straight line to success. But there is a fundamental flaw to siding with Achilles over our rationality: Achilles is not only a mythological character—he is half-god. That seems like a light-hearted, absurdly obvious statement, but I think we need to remind ourselves of that occasionally. We have a force within us in the form of the superego that tells us to transcend our mortality to achieve success. Talk about a weight on your shoulders!

It is so much easier to succeed when no one, including yourself, is expecting you to succeed. Even in this paper, I write hesitantly, critically, and loathingly, thinking that I can't possibly live up to the superlative compliment I received from Professor Valenza in class. It's a harsh paradox, because that was the best compliment I have ever received, and it brought me to tears. Yet the minute I got it, I thought, "What I am going to write about to top this?" and immediately started dwelling over this added pressure. I laugh at the irony, because I remember hearing Professor Valenza's story about receiving tenure and having a similar feeling, and thinking to myself, "Wow, if that ever happens to me, I will stop working then and there." But we don't stop working; he didn't, I won't. We never do.

When French aristocrat Alexis De Tocqueville visited America in the early 1800s, he marveled at the value Americans put on material wealth. He said material consumption was our outlet for our precious right of the pursuit of happiness. Americans are ostentatiously wealthy; we use our material wealth to flaunt our monetary success, and many people derive their happiness from that "success." While the need to validate one's happiness with a show of wealth might be characteristically American, the need to legitimize one's joy with the laud of another is innately human.

Right after I freaked out over the expectations of my final paper, I called my mom to tell her what happened. Nearly shaking in anticipation as I dialed, I was heartbroken when no one answered the phone. I called her office, her cell phone. No answer. Suddenly I sunk into a slump. It was as if all the joy I had just experienced was wiped from my memory, as if it had never happened if I couldn't share it with her. I couldn't understand why I couldn't be happy with just the self-satisfaction. Why did I need someone else to validate this feeling? As I thought about this question, I remembered our discussion of the coherence theory of truth, which says—and this is an admittedly simplistic characterization—that reality is merely a societal consensus. If the correspondence theory were applied to my experience to access its "reality," it would deem the emotions real because my classmates and professor were present to validate the experience; however, the feeling did not climax until I spoke to my mom. Akin to Cash's relationship with his mother Addie in William Faulkner's *As I Lay Dying*, I realized that I ground certain truths in my mother, and one of those truths is "success." Her approval of my actions is so dire to my happiness because I equate it with success. Perhaps seeking that kind of approval is another aspect of the immaturity that Salinger writes about. Maturity is being able to feel success independently of judgment or corroboration.

Along with *kleos* and the superego, familial approval motivates our drive for success. Franz Kafka's *The Metamorphosis* illustrates how familial neglect can ultimately be fatal. The protagonist and breadwinner in the Samsa family, Gregor, incapacitated by his abrupt transformation into an insect, is virtually disowned by his family when he cannot continue supporting them. Gregor desperately tries to win back their affection by returning to work despite his circumstances—yet another example of human drive to defy our own abilities—but inevitably fails, as he has lost his human form. Ironically, the insect Gregor exhibits the truest form of humanity: he is imbued with the tenacious pursuit of a not only elusive, but utterly unattainable success.

The *Bhagavad-Gita* tells us to act with detachment: "Be intent on action, not the fruits of action." Of all the works and theories we have studied this year, this one is the hardest for me to grasp. I don't think I require any more praise for my actions than anyone else, but I simply cannot "be impartial to success and failure." I am too passionate about everything I do to be indifferent to the results. Achilles, the ardent demigod, devoted his life to *kleos*. Irrational, rash, and infinitely bold, Achilles acted without regard to consequence, yet he did not "do good and disappear." His actions were entirely motivated by his desire for *kleos*.

Last summer I visited the Isabella Stuart Gardner Museum in Boston and saw an exhibit by a resident artist. He was given a medium-sized room, all the supplies he requested, and a year's stay, and was told to "make art on the walls." The catch, however, was that whatever he did, at the end of the year, would be exhibited for a certain amount of time, and then destroyed. The walls would be painted over, and prepared for the next resident artist. When I heard this, I was horrified. I thought how could someone possibly devote an entire year of his or her life to something he or she knew was going to be destroyed? When I visited the exhibit, the feelings were even more compelling. I was brought to tears knowing that all the meticulous detail, the experiences of the artist, the emotional responses the work was eliciting within me at that very moment, the visual documentation of that moment in my life, all would be destroyed. I realized that going into that room I had more at stake than I have ever had viewing art. I knew that it was my one and only chance to have the experience, and that made the experience so much more poignant. There are probably hundreds of works I have seen around the world to which I will never have the privilege of returning, but no work has struck me or will ever strike as deeply as the one that I knew would disappear. That memory showed me that doing good and disappearing does not compromise success. To me, that artist achieved *kleos*.

My experiences lead me to a definition of success not as a painful cycle of disappointments, not as a straight arrow to achievement, but as a convoluted path. While I have not reached a definition of success that I can completely comprehend, let alone a universal statement about success, I know that the philosopher Robin Hartshorne comes close when he speaks of the priority of beauty. Success is beauty, but I would add that seeing the beauty on the path is even more successful.

THE IMPASSE

....

Colin McDonell

IN CLASS LAST WEEK, during our analysis of Dostoyevsky's *The Grand Inquisitor*, we considered the Grand Inquisitor's assertion that God was wrong in allowing us the ability to commit evil. This struck a strong chord with me, as I have long been of the belief that it is fundamentally impossible for a God both omnipotent and benevolent to exist when such evil exists in the world, evil that would theoretically be in his power to stop. I therefore agreed that if God did exist he should have secured mankind's happiness by preventing evil. Being omnipotent, this is in his power, and being benevolent, this is in his interests. Chelsea Norell, a classmate of religious conviction, disagreed, and this led into a debate which continued days after class let out. Although I still disagree with her conclusion, I came to understand much of her reasoning as to why she believes God was correct in allowing evil in the world. Our discussion came to an impasse when we discovered the ultimate root of our disagreement: her acceptance and my rejection of faith.

Seeing the existence of evil in the world and the existence of an all-powerful and perfect God as mutually exclusive, I naturally agreed that if God did exist, he would prevent us from doing evil and rightfully so. If man were stripped of his ability to kill, for instance, then such atrocities as genocide, war, and murder would no longer exist on earth. Few would argue that the world is a better place without these things, and it isn't difficult to take the logic of this sentiment a step further and to assert that the world would be better off if man couldn't kill. In taking such steps to remove evil, God would at worst merely lessen the amount of suffering on earth or at best create a utopian society in which all are happy. In using "utopian," I don't mean to imply an endorsement of some sort of communist or socialist government, as I am utterly opposed to such limitations on my freedom by other mere mortals. In this hypothetical, it is a perfect and all-knowing God making the decisions, so the context is entirely different. In any case, a world in which God prevents evil by any degree seems preferable to one in which he doesn't.

Chelsea nonetheless argued utterly against God stripping man of the ability to commit evil. She argued that if man were prevented from committing acts of evil, he would essentially be stripped of his freewill and individuality. I disagree. It isn't a question of limiting will to do evil, but the *capability* to do evil. For example, God could have prevented murder by designing man without the physical characteristics necessary to kill another man or without the mental capacity to fathom murder. Just because man lacks the ability to fathom all possible thoughts or to carry out all possible actions, it doesn't follow that he lacks freewill. Man currently lacks the ability to levitate on command or solve certain scientific mysteries, and yet we still say man possesses freewill.

Chelsea argued furthermore that if God started by just preventing men from killing, this policy could be extended until every possible choice would be analyzed as more or less evil, with men being thereby reduced to puppets whose every action is dictated by God. This statement entirely depends on what view of God one accepts. In most major religions, God specifically spells out what evil is in commandments and such. If one accepts this view of God, then man would not be reduced to mere puppet because only these actions would be prevented, leaving choice in a multitude of other matters. However, this isn't the only view of God, and so I believe that her overall point remains valid. All actions could potentially be appraised as more or less evil and the removal of man's capability to take the slightly more evil course of action in all circumstances would essentially strip him of freewill. I still argue that this situation would be preferable to the current, for although lacking freewill, men would be happy. (Here I must admit that I agree with the Grand Inquisitor.) Since we use freewill as a means to attain happiness, if we were already given happiness, freewill would lose its point and become unnecessary.

Here Chelsea brought up a point I had never before fully considered. She stated her belief that God created men so that they would glorify him and freewill is necessary for them to do so. She believes that man glorifies God through good deeds and by utilizing God-given talents, and only by having the option of choosing between good and evil can man truly glorify God by actually *choosing* good instead of simply having no other option than doing good. This logic makes sense to me. However, it doesn't seem to me that if God is perfect he would need any external reassurance of it, especially reassurance by such relatively inferior mortals. It makes even less sense that he would create a world that would unnecessarily glorify him when it would cost so much in human suffering. If external glorification is unnecessary, it would seem an act of malevolence of God to inflict man with war and genocide in order to gain something he doesn't even need. In her response to this, Chelsea explained that glorification is more than just a "pat on the back" for God. By glorifying God through good deeds and intellectual discovery we allow mankind to progress and become better and happier. Without this option civilization would be stagnant. I agree, but as I stated earlier, I believe stagnancy is not, in this case, a bad thing. Such a civilization would be stagnant because it is already happy, and in fact our current civilization strives for this happy, and therefore ultimately stagnant, state. Since this is what we strive for, we certainly don't truly consider it to be a bad thing. I also pointed out that God could have filled the world with even more evil, which would set us at a lower level and give us even more to strive for, but certainly no one would advocate a world filled with more death and destruction just for this.

Here we arrive at the impasse. Chelsea replied that she believes God chose the degree of evil in the world for reasons she is unable to comprehend, and she believes these reasons are correct as a matter of faith. Although in this essay I attempted to organize the exchange between Chelsea and me in a logical flow with the impasse at the end, in reality the subject of faith entered our discussion much earlier. For example, I asked why God couldn't have designed our bodies so that we required less food to sustain ourselves or so that we weren't susceptible to cancer, measures that in no way infringe upon freewill but would lessen human suffering. To this Chelsea responded that she didn't know, but believed on faith that God had just reason to do so. Thus insofar as a theist accepts God's existence on faith, the theist must necessarily also defend God's actions on faith, at least in certain matters. But I reject the use of faith in this connection and believe that if a benevolent God existed, he would remove evil from the world on grounds of logical consistency alone. But is this belief of mine itself an act of faith, perhaps of another sort? Whatever the case, our arguments are contingent on the validity of faith itself, a subject far too broad to broach in this essay. Thus the impasse must remain until a future discussion or essay attempts to break it down.

LIFE AS A SONATA

Miyabe Yu

ARISTOTLE UNDERSTANDS THAT EVERY object has a function, and by fulfilling its function, it attains happiness. For example, a hammer's function is to hammer; if a hammer cannot hammer, the hammer is not fulfilling its function, and therefore it is no longer a hammer. This statement suggests that there is meaning to life. Throughout history brave thinkers, such as Socrates, Aristotle, and Freud, have sought to determine what justifies the existence of human beings. Why do I wake up every morning? Why do I challenge myself to live this life? Such questions underestimate why human beings form relationships and strive for an identity. Even as selfish creatures, every person's deed greatly impacts others. There is a greater function for human beings than survival. Along the lines of the slogan, "The children are the future of the world," every person is responsible for the future. The modern world is a result of history, and history is an ultimate result of every person's existence, a vast mosaic of minute tiles. And yet, to extend the metaphor, the pattern that these tiles make collectively does not belong to any one of them. Wars, peace, inventions and continued human existence do not happen because of one sole person.

If life were a matter of meaningless coincidences, then there would be no need to form an identity or relationships. Most emphatically, this is not the case. For example, during 9/11, one of the hijacked planes crashed into Stanley Praimnath's office at the eighty-first-floor South Tower. The crash created a debris wall that blocked Mr. Praimnath from the exit. Coincidentally, a man named Brian Clark heard Mr. Praimnath's cry while he was descending down the emergency stairs. He valiantly stopped, went in, and helped Mr. Praimnath tear down the wall of debris. They then exited the building seconds before the tower collapsed. This story makes me rethink the importance of one person's life to another. If Brian Clark were not there and had not acted, Stanley Praimnath would not be alive today.

Freud and Hobbes seem to believe that people are constantly self-serving beings. Nevertheless there are actual people who "do good and disappear." For example, in Malta there are a lot of stray cats. Every morning, while my family and I waited for our tour bus, we would play with these cats. At times I would sneak some salami from the continental breakfast but, to my disappointment, the cats would never eat it. One day, a man came by with a large plastic bag filled with cat food and started to feed the thirty-or-so cats at once. Later that year, there was a television documentary about this so-called Catman. The TV crew interviewed several people who said that the Catman buys the cat food, out of his own salary, simply because he loves cats. The Catman offers his money and labor for love, and we should learn from him that sometimes helping others provides greater personal satisfaction than seeking to fulfill our personal needs. We should learn to love and to live with each other with simple acts of caring. And each of us becomes a moral person not by a single action, but by a series of actions performed by a person who understands the point of doing it—much as a musician demonstrates her accomplishment not with a single note, but with a series of notes that she understands and interprets.

Tolstoy shows us how Ivan Ilych suffers a lonely death because he believed that reputation and possessions were the only keys to happiness. However, people can easily train themselves to attain these things, and still be unhappy. Nowadays the standard education system and economic environment make it all too easy to be successful in this simplistic sense. The system favors the survival of the fittest by glorifying merit via competition. I am also guilty of taking part in this current phenomenon. My life has been full of competitions ever since I was born. Whether it was the fine arts or physique, I often saw myself striving to be the best. But then there is the example of Franny from *Franny and Zooey*: Franny and her boyfriend seem to exemplify the true American Dream of imminent successful achievement, and yet Franny is still insecure about her way of living. Despite her enormous talent as an actress, she refuses to give in to the rewards of inauthenticity. People too often do not consider the consequences of achieving apparently selfish, but ultimately externally driven desires. We often misread happiness as equivalent to the attainment of status, whether as a matter of material possessions or intangible acknowledgments, or both. But such acquisitive pleasures are short-lived and do not bring contentment in life. Pleasure-seeking is what animals do, and should not be what human beings want.

There is a stereotype that Asian parents are academically strict and prudent, and yet I believe this statement to be biased. Success is important, but my parents value my efforts more than my grades. This is why I believe that my existence cannot be merely a product of society's pressures and expectations. The direction of my life seems questionable at times, and I think I am too judgmental at eighteen years old. I came to the United States at the age of fourteen, covered in my mother's tears. I studied hard in high school, won awards, made friends and applied to college. I was accepted by and enrolled in my first choice, and now I am going into my second year. Why did I choose to live such a systematic life? It's funny how *Questions of Civilization* has altered how I view my life. I had assumed that it would proceed in the spectacular style of Achilles, but now it seems to have transformed itself into the more modest style of Odysseus.

High accolades are good but can simultaneously blind people to their true desires. Sometimes when things are going too well, I want simply to keep them moving in the same direction without considering what lies beyond. Nevertheless, I emphatically agree with Socrates that "the unexamined life is not worth living," because otherwise one ceases to understand one's own actions, and such understanding is necessary to be rational and good. Without self-examination one may well approach the presumed "good life" as somehow lying in opposition to just living life authentically. One does not find truth.

With new medicines, equipment and knowledge, modern technology has the capability of significantly improving and prolonging the life of a human being. However, there are still people who want to commit suicide or simply cannot find meaning in life. For them, life is a prison that offers no exits; it seems impossible to escape from the apparent absurdity of things. They languish and lament and find no song to sing.

We must all carefully observe our own faults and limitations before we can be balanced, happy and filled with song. By facing our faults and continuously practicing improvement, we build the courage and the vision to see and to share life's beauty. The process is similar to making music on a violin. A violin is a very fragile instrument, a piece of consummately delicate craftsmanship. It needs constant attention and good care to create bravura music. Moreover, once a violinist begins a piece of music, he must engage it without reservation and play the entire composition to bring about its true magnificence. So, too, must we approach our lives as we would a violin: to listen, to practice, to play—and to adore.

ON THE PREVIOUS PAGE is a poem that I wrote last semester, after I had quit believing in souls. I remember that when I wrote this poem, I had just read a poem by a famous author that moved me and inspired me to create my own piece; but as I started thinking about what to write, I realized that I hadn't written in months. I decided that I had stopped writing because I stopped letting myself express my emotions in art, so I wrote a poem about the conflict between the part of my personality that creates and the part of my personality that suppresses creation. It may seem strange that any part of me would want to suppress creativity, but I have learned that the drive that creates art takes time and energy—and my more logical mind thinks that all of my time and energy should be dedicated to excelling in work or school. When I was younger I thought I could excel by doing art, but I have learned that poets don't always do well in life, and I want to do well in life.

So I don't write as often as I used to, and so I don't write as well as I used to, and that is what inspired this poem—but I don't think that a soul is required to create or enjoy art.

Then what is the purpose of art for the purely physical, soulless human being? I like to think that Darwin would have an answer—and I have a few ideas about the evolution of art—but when it comes right down to it, neither do I know nor do I care whether or not science alone explains the existence of art. I am content to separate the logical and scientific from the creative and artistic in my mind and in my life, just as I did in this poem.

Discovering Meaning in Life through the Existence of a Higher Spirit

Annelise Reynolds

At the very beginning of this course we were asked whether we preferred the world of *Genesis* or the world of the Big Bang. Without thinking, I was more inclined to agree with the Big Bang theory. The idea of some god randomly deciding to create our world in such a simple manner, or why he came up with the world as we know it as opposed to some other completely different world with different mathematical equations—or even none at all—didn't sound reasonable to me. "And God said, 'let there be light'; and there was light. And God saw that the light was good..." I have always thought of religion as an easily accessible backbone of support for people without confidence. Not to mention, I have had such persecutory encounters with extremely religious people in the past that I have always held religion in contempt as a manifestation of a person's intolerances.

But then I was asked to consider a difficult theoretical situation: A messenger (who knows the truth for a fact and whose message is verified), walks into the room and announces that God does not exist. I was asked to think about how that would make me feel. After thinking for a couple seconds, I couldn't even fathom how I would feel if there was no God, and unknowingly avoided the question by declaring that there was no way that anybody could ever know this for a fact. Obviously, Mr. Valenza challenged me again by dismissing the possible flaws of the hypothetical question and to focus more on what he was really asking, but my brain refused to consider it. No matter how much he challenged me to think about the question rather than the actual possibility, I couldn't wrap my mind around the idea that God does not exist. After several minutes of this debate, Mr. Valenza gave up asking me and said: "When you reach a point where nobody can convince you otherwise—where nothing can count as evidence against your position—you've reached a core belief."

I sat thinking for a couple minutes, removed from the discussion, and pondered Mr. Valenza's statement. Could that be true, that I so deeply believed in some godly form that it was an unquestionable part of my being? The answer was, and still is, "Yes!" I realized that day that I did believe in some higher power. I wrote both my teacher's quote and my response—"God, or some greater energy, exists"—in my notebook. The fact that I was slightly surprised at my innate response to Mr. Valenza's questions, and that I was surprised in my apparent certain belief in god, also revealed to me that I had never dug deep enough into my own thoughts to figure out why I believed certain things, or even what I believed. Not bad for the first day of class.

Having established that I did believe in god from the first reading, the second reading followed pace and helped me examine why. Class discussions infused with atheistic and existential comments in response to Sybil's behavior in *You Shall Know Them* frankly made me cringe slightly on the inside. I have always tried to remain objective and see any situation from all points of view in order to avoid the trap of intolerance that I suffered from when I was younger. Yet I had a difficult time listening to some of my classmate Colin's comments because everything in me was screaming to deny what he was saying. He declared that we are nothing more than matter, and that what we classify as the soul is simply a series of chemical reactions to which we attach a certain meaning.

Every fiber in me wanted to avoid really thinking about what Colin was saying. I did not want to allow his thoughts to seep into my mind, for I was afraid of them. Admitting that there is no higher power, or even anything beyond tangible matter, meant that I was nothing. "I can't be nothing," I thought. "I make choices; decide my movements and my actions. I am me, how can I not exist?" Essentially, I had reached the point at which Descartes declared: "I think, therefore I am."

This struggle also solidified my belief in a more dualistic type of world. I agree with the laws of science and believe in exploration and questioning; yet I do not think that human capabilities are sufficient to handle metaphysical questions. If we only believe what can be proven, we choose to ignore some of the miraculous or bizarre occurrences in this world. That we simply don't understand something doesn't mean it cannot be true. Who are we to assume that we are all-knowing? Even though mankind has thus far been unsuccessful in proving that something beyond the purely physical exists, this does not signify that it does not. Rather—although it could be true—humans may simply be incapable of examining such an insurmountable idea.

Because I personally believe in a world spirit-energy, I also believe that everything is interconnected; in order to better know its beauty, one must strive to know and experience as much of it as is possible. That is what gives meaning to my life. I try to educate myself, try new experiences, delight in my different emotions, and accept all that I encounter, for everything is one small part of an infinitely large energy. I picture this spirit as never-ending, constantly changing, and constantly flowing. I don't believe in a religious type of black-and-white "good" and "evil," or "God" and "Devil," but that they are combined. The lines of good and evil are blurred.

This energy is not the stereotypical type of God that sits above our world and watches, judging our every move and influencing the outcome of events. To the contrary, because it is an ever-moving flow of energy, it is unconcerned with every-day trivial events. It wouldn't manipulate the natural flow of the world to create unnatural outcomes. This explains the randomness and injustice of the world. We are but one microscopic part of a universally large flow.

I am not religious; I am spiritual. I don't follow anybody else's beliefs, so I maintain my independence and avoid feeling brainwashed, but also enjoy the comfort of metaphysical support. I must admit again that I am not strong enough, or disenfranchised enough with the magic of life, to believe in a world without something else to it than what we can see. I may be wrong, but this is how I am choosing my path in life, so what does it matter if it keeps me sane and happy. At this point I would choose to be naive and happy rather than right and disheartened with life.

Often people confuse religion and spirituality. True religious people follow some doctrine of established rules and beliefs. To many religious people life is largely just a vessel to the eternal afterlife. They would rather look for the beauty of God than the beauty around them now. Many are so closed-minded and dogmatic about beliefs they were taught—beliefs that are by no means necessarily inherent in the world—that they miss out on so many of the interesting and beautiful aspects of life in order to stay within the narrow confines of their religious lifestyle.

I see the beautiful things in the world as part of the eternal spirit's magic. In order to know this energy and to live life to fulfill its meaning we must explore as much of it as we can. I find meaning in exploring the world, enjoying all that it has to offer, and connecting with it. Confucius couldn't be farther from my personal beliefs. The point he most strongly pushes is filial piety. I agree that this is important; just as important as maintaining healthy and active relationships. However, I view relationships and respect among people as something that is innate. Connection with others is another form of connection with the whole world spirit (eternal spirit, world spirit—I don't know how else to call such an unknowable, grandiose thing) that we are all a part of. They should be such an integrated part of our lives that we don't have to focus on them or make them the purpose of our lives.

Confucius also encourages people to just accept what is passed down to them, continue with life as it has been done for years, and maintain the soft rigidity of manners. Basically: thinking = creating = bad? NO! ABSOLUTELY NOT! Life should be lived in a tempered (once again I am referring to an Odyssean mean) Marianne of *Sense and Sensibility* style. I want to live my life by experiencing many things. Emotions and thoughts are one of the most direct ways to access this worldly energy, so denying them would be to miss out on an opportunity to bathe in the sacred purpose of our physical world. Of course our emotions should not be allowed to rule us, but they most certainly should not be ignored. Instead, they should be explored productively, such as via art. Questioning and sampling the world in a philosophical manner is my "engaged virtue."

There are many ways via which we can explore the world: physical laws via science, emotion and feeling via art, thoughts and ideas via philosophy and literature, or connection via relationships. Our lives should be a combination of all of these adventures. I do believe that there is some higher order of which we are all a part. In order to be as much as possible an integrated part of the natural flow of the world, we should try to learn all we can and refuse inactivity. "The unexamined life is not worth living." This world is here as a part of the greater spirit; if we want to connect to it, we should try to experience as much of it as we can.

As such a miniscule part of an unfathomable large deity, I shall never know its full extents—nor should I. Via my belief in the kind of higher spirit that I have described, I find meaning and purpose in my life by experiencing and questioning as much of everything as possible...

Not the truth in whose possession some human being is or thinks he is, but the honest trouble he has taken to get behind the truth is what constitutes the worth of a human being....

If God held in his closed right hand all truth and in his left hand only the ever live drive for truth, albeit with the addition that I should always and evermore err, and he said to me: Choose! I should humbly grab his left hand, saying: Father, give! Pure truth is after all for you alone!

—Gotthold Efraim Lessing
(translated by Walter Kaufmann)

THE CREATION AND INTERPRETATION OF ART

Mangalvar

LEO TOLSTOY STATED IN his work *What is Art?* "…many things, the production of which does not afford pleasure to the producer and the sensation received from which is unpleasant…may nevertheless be undoubted works of art." With this definition in mind, the untitled poem below that I wrote for this assignment is undeniably art. Although it was extremely unpleasant to write, nearly brought me to tears, and left me in a bitter mood, I created a piece of artwork that revealed my inner thoughts and feelings better than facial expressions or conversations. The creation of art is arguably the most cathartic activity in which one can engage. As one creates art, it is almost as if one's feelings are transmitted from her body onto the canvas or paper.

The poem I wrote was extremely negative, although this was not my original intention. The feelings of despair, worthlessness, and confusion appear to infect the reader, and this supports the argument that my poem is art. Art is intended to fill the reader with the feelings the author felt as he or she created the work; and although I do not think—from my observations and conversations with readers of the poem—that my poem can or should fully achieve this goal, it does appear to impact readers on a negative emotional level. Although my feelings of pain and suffering may have been embellished by my pen, everyone who reads my poem can relate to the emotions it conveys to some degree, and thus in a sense are living through my experiences.

In my search for artistic inspiration I explored paintings, music, and written art forms. Via this exploration, I found that for me the most inspirational and touching type of art was music. As I listened to various songs, I realized that I attached specific memories to certain of them. Not only can song lyrics be related to experiences and feelings, but when you hear a song during an intense emotional episode or period, hearing the song at a later time can have a powerful emotional response. Thus I can find more songs that evoke strong emotions than paintings because music is often playing in the background as memories are formed. The songs I associate with memories from my first semester of college mainly evoke feelings of regret, thus the inspiration for my poem. This semester was filled with many joyful moments, but for me it is easier to recall an extremely painful memory than one which is blissful.

I believe also that people experience different degrees of emotional response to different artistic mediums. As a musician, I have the strongest emotional response to music as opposed to my roommate, who is a painter and considers visual art of a superior quality. I am not a visual person, so brushstrokes have far less of an emotional impact on me than notes or words. I realize that a bold, dark brush stroke can convey great emotion, but for me the word "livid" or the jarring sound of a gong are much less ambiguous and thus hold greater emotional value for the observer. Whether I am cheerful or upset, I am more able to channel these feelings into the intonation in a piece of music or the words of a poem than the brushstrokes on a canvas.

While walking back from the Pomona Art Gallery, after observing many paintings and pictures, I realized that the words of the songs to which I was listening had a far more stirring effect than the paintings and sculptures I had gazed at moments before. Although those works were of a high quality, I found them harder to enjoy than music because of the environment in which they were housed. Art must be enjoyed at one's own pace in a personal environment. It is impossible to block out the sounds of the strange electronic music in the Pomona Art Gallery or the accusatory glances from the security guard. It is even harder to ignore the descriptions next to the paintings and sculptures and to prevent them from altering your interpretation of the art. It is much easier to slip on a pair of noise-canceling headphones, close your eyes, and fully enjoy the art of sound, than it is to remove a painting from an art gallery and bring it to a secluded, peaceful environment where it can be properly interpreted and enjoyed.

I chose not to title my poem because I feel as if a title limits the reader's emotional response. By leaving the subject open to interpretation, the reader can better interpret its artistic value. The best art does not directly implant ideas in the reader, but rather presents an open canvas onto which the reader can pour his or her emotional response.

UNTITLED
by Mangalvar

I turn up the volume to try to drown my thoughts
They never stop keeping me up at night
Never stop diverting my attention away from the brighter things
    in life
I focus on the lyrics; the thoughts swirling through my mind fade
    into the background
Then reappear tenfold
The music controls the volume of my thoughts
Increasing or decreasing their intensity
Eventually the volume is too much, and the thoughts creep
Back into my mind like a toxin.
Alcohol blurs my judgments, numbs my mind.
Slows my thoughts, eases the pain
My tongue becomes looser
My thoughts begin to trickle out of my mouth
Then flow, spill, gush.
Gush, spill, flow, trickle.
My thoughts spin more slowly, reform
The pain returns, the confusion, the loneliness.
His empty touch clears my head temporarily.
Nights of kisses that mean nothing.
Deceptive gazes and words that charm but remain vacant
"You are more to me than..."
I'm nothing to you. Just a body to hold for the night and discard
    the next morning.
My thoughts remain tucked away until the temporary high wears
    off
And the truth becomes clear.

POEM

E. Madison Shimoda

the waiting
the unshed tears
the thorn on the rose
the carpet under your feet
the mournful howl of a widow
the Maha Mayas and Virgin Marys
the tired horse watching over her colt
the dream left to be unexperienced forever
the hot bruises and scars of domestic violence
the billboard of half-nakedness posing for cigarettes
the spent body on a motel bed, wondering what had just happened
the hand washing clothes in the cold stream by the urine-stenched gutters
the girl who lets men call her bitch, c--t, slut, whore because her mother was called so
the voluptuous body saying hey baby but thinking what the hell am I doing?
the overstretched opening; in pain but too afraid to complain
the creator of many miracles that is never given credit
the patience and endurance of those before me
the stomach that has starved for centuries
the instrument that is soundless
the lips that are stitched shut
the underpaid soldier
the best friend
the daughter
the mother
the sister
the wife
Woman

THE JOURNEY TO DENIAL

Gloria Diaz

DO YOU BELIEVE IN God? This is a question that has slowly dawned in my life and gradually become one of more and more ambiguity and importance. As a child, this question did not exist, but now as a freshman in college enrolled in this particular civilization class, it haunts my thoughts.

Growing up in a Mexican Catholic household, I was raised to be just as fervent a believer in God as my parents. My childhood consisted of baptism, first communion, confirmation, going to church every Sunday, attending the weekly meeting of the Catholic youth groups, going to Catholic retreats, and praying every night before going to sleep. I truly did believe that, "In the beginning God created the heavens and the earth." (*Genesis*) My mother taught me to believe that "male and female he created them, and he blessed them," and that being so, I should be thankful to Him and I should adore

Him and comply with His commands. God was always my refuge; I would go to him for everything. I was a devoted child. However, due to several incidents that have occurred in my life, my faith and belief in God and His existence has slowly faded. By my senior year in high school, I had already declared to myself that I did not believe in God. I had stopped going to church, stopped praying, and stopped restricting myself from what He and the church would call sin. I believed as Sybil in *You Shall Know Them*, "that this life depend[ed] so utterly on me, on me alone...on my sole judgment." Thus a question that did not even exist for the child acquired an obvious answer for the high school senior. Now as a freshman in college, and part of this civilization class, I have begun again to examine my beliefs.

Genesis, You Shall Know Them, and the discussion of the hypothetical question, "What would we do if someone came in and notified you that it had been proven that God doesn't exist?" are three factors that made me reexamine my stand on the existence of God.

When I first got here, I had no doubt in my mind that God did not exist, and so I was not very happy about the assignment to read *Genesis*. I thought it would be a complete waste of time. As I was reading the text, it was a little surprising to see that I began to have mixed feelings. Some parts reminded me of what I believed as a child; some reinforced the reasons why I do not believe in God; others made me think that my position of disbelief might be wrong. I was raised to believe that God is all-powerful and generous and deserves our worship, but now I cannot agree that such a description would apply to someone who has the heart or the right to punish us with all the cruel things that happen on earth. As *Genesis* depicts, God gave Adam a horrible punishment: "Cursed is the ground because of you; through painful toil you will eat of it all the days of your life." To Eve he said, "I will greatly increase your pains in childbearing; with pain you will give birth to children. Your desire will be for your husband, and he will rule over you." This portrayal of God in *Genesis* is of something that cannot be a God to me. From this, I realized that I refuse to worship and believe in the existence of such a being because, in my eyes, a God cannot wish badly upon anyone. I can neither adore nor forgive someone who really is responsible for the suffering of humanity. And yet, when I read, "the lord saw that the wickedness of man was great in the earth... the Lord was sorry that he had made man on the earth, and it grieved him to his heart," for an instant, I thought that maybe humans were the evil ones and that God did exist and that we were a disappointment to him just as sometimes we are disappointed with the things that *we* create. But consider: He is not just one of us; He is the almighty God, and being so, He should have foreseen what He had brought forth, and He should have been able to repair His creation, to have made us as good as He wanted us to be, rather than cursing us. Thus while *Genesis* managed to make me doubt my atheism in several instances, ultimately, as a whole, it sounded like a fiction written to create the fear of God in people and thereby to regulate their behavior. I remained in denial, and the next reading took me yet further in this direction.

Elements of the novel *You Shall Know Them*, by Vercors, brought me to a stronger stand on the nonexistence of God. As a child, I was taught that we are all his creations and that he loves us all the same. In *You Shall Know Them*, it seemed that the teachings about God are contradictory. Therefore, when I read in connection with the *tropis*, "but if they are beasts, Douglas, you couldn't think of giving them the sacrament! It would be an ungodly act!" I once again thought that God could not possibly exist. If He created everything on earth, therefore also the animals, He should love them, too. Therefore it should not be "ungodly" to bless a creature whether it be human or not. Nevertheless, the mentality portrayed in the book is the same as in many religious societies of today. I was, moreover, influenced by Sybil's existentialism. When I read Sybil's statement, "nothing ever comes to guide us," I became even more convinced that God does not exist. The line made me remember that all of my childhood I prayed to God incessantly and the only thing that came to guide me were imperfect human beings just like me, but with more experience. Never did any godly creature step in to help me or get me out of a bad situation. Sybil adds, nonetheless, "The heavens are empty... But though you know it's so, you still can't get used to it." At this I became aware that some of my actions—actions which I further questioned the next day during class discussion—are not those of an atheist.

What would we do if someone came in and notified you that it had been proven that God does not exist? For almost a year, I had been almost completely sure that I did not believe in God up until the moment this questioned was asked. The first thing that came into my mind was my second quote from Sybil, and how, in my case, it is true. Even though I have not believed in God for almost two years now, I still "speak" to Him. Sometimes I find myself lonely and in need of speaking with someone. I talk in my head but refer to whom I am "speaking" as God. There is no kind of worshipping in this conversation, or praying, or even less pleading; it is just as though I were talking to anybody else, or to myself. It sounds silly, but He has become my friend, and I sometimes "speak" to Him because I can say anything, and He will neither tell anybody nor judge me—because really I am just talking to myself. My excuse for this behavior has been that I like to lie to myself and that I like the idea that there could be someone there listening, but hearing the question and recalling my feelings during the readings, the doubt came into me that maybe there is an element of hope behind it, or another reason. But as I processed the idea, I realized that when I think of Him, I feel resentful. My life has been a series of unfortunate and painful events over the course of which I have *not* experienced the presence of God. After so many years that I spent being loyal to Him and going to Him for answers, I feel that even so He never protected me, but instead, left me to be vulnerable to all the evil He brought upon us. Perhaps it is not healthy to continue talking to a presence that I hold as neither existent nor worthy of my worship, and to pretend that He is listening. The only explanation I can find after all the self-examination brought about by the readings and discussion is that I have given up in frustration. I would rather believe that He does not exist than to take on the disappointment that God really is one who is evil or merely indifferent to our suffering; that He offers no remedies and no protection for the curse He has brought upon us.

The combination of *Genesis*, *You Shall Know Them*, and the question in our discussion made me realize my real position regarding my belief in God, and the reasons behind it. As a child, God was an all-powerful, generous, kind, and perfect being, and as I grew and became aware of all the cruel things in the world—and in particular in *my* world—I can neither see the possibility of His existence nor accept another description for Him.

CONSEQUENCE OF CONFORMITY

Tammy Nguyen

FROM THE START, WE have been taught that for every action we take, there exists a consequence that can be either detrimental or beneficial. Thus, as children, we often found ourselves restricted within limitations that society deemed necessary to maintain its own, less cosmological version of *logos*, or the design and harmony that we discussed early on in *Questions of Civilization*. Much of our learning spent in classrooms has taught us that we must control our urges by logically reasoning before acting. Since we are taught to monitor our actions, is it possible that we limit our potential by molding ourselves into the ideal citizens that society so highly praises? In society, there is order in almost every aspect of life, from the manners that govern the way we eat our meals to the appropriate choice of colors to paint a building. Is our experience limited by this obsessive need to organize every aspect of the world? Or are we better off with this communal conformity to an ideal?

Lao-Tzu in the *Tao Te Ching* states that "Names can name no lasting name." His poetic words lament how naming can take away from our perception of the world, limiting our experience and sense of mystery by constraining how we see and what we remember of a specific object, place, or person. I believe, too, that the constraints within society *do* limit how we perceive our environment, and perhaps the biggest skewing of our perception indeed has its cause in our system of naming. For example, I was told that the ocean was blue before I ever laid my eyes on it, so when I did see it, my observation was already predetermined by what society had told me. In every piece of art I painted, water was automatically blue because I had been trained to think so, and thus I never chose to paint it green or purple. The way we name colors limits how we perceive the world; it gives us initial boundaries which restrain us from creating our own names and our own untainted observations. Professor Valenza told us in class how he was severely reprimanded in kindergarten for coloring the sky purple when he could find no blue crayon. Though the mistake was so minis-cule and apparently forgivable, I think that the consequences were large. This kind of correction leaves the impression that art is not about personal expression, but about following the standards set by society in yet another domain. There are certain absolute truths, or facts, that govern our world and reflect our need to categorize the world around us, and these extend from mere crayon colors to matters such as ethnicity.

> *A black man said to a white man: "When I'm born, I'm black. When I'm embarrassed, I'm black. When I'm sick, I'm black. When I'm hot, I'm black. When I'm cold, I'm black. But you? When you're born, you're purple. When you're embarrassed, you're pink. When you're sick, you're green. When you're hot, you're red. And when you're cold, you're blue. So who are you to call me colored?"*

Though this story is obviously an exaggerated overstatement, the ste-reotyping resulting from our necessity for classification has had horrible consequences at times. Our naming system has failed us severely when, as a people, we find it difficult to tolerate and understand alien cultures. This pursuit of order and structure has created preconceived notions within individuals, depriving them of the opportunity to create their own opinions, and thus manipulating their experiences. Thus, we have been left with a society that battles with misconceptions and exhibits xenophobic tendencies. Perhaps Sigmund Freud's main thesis in *Civilization and Its Discontents* has its place in today's society because it seems that civilization *does* injure one's psyche. Society teaches a set of principles that members adopt from childhood, but this unconditional acceptance restricts our ability to shape our own beliefs, and thus "civilizing" the human being may indeed be more of a hindrance than a service.

Genesis is the perfect example of how society can limit us. Within this first book of the Holy Bible, God, a supreme being, creates and controls with boundaries and structure. There is water and land, night and day, and organization in every creation. The control under which each part of this world is molded reflects the rigid regulations that manage present-day society. Religious believers are highly swayed by the teachings of the Bible in the same way that citizens are manipulated by social standards. By learning to accept the regulations placed upon us since birth, we forfeit our ability to have full control of every decision and every thought because each experience was skewed by some prior phase of indoctrination. This power that we allow to persuade our every action has left us to become identical cookies cut by a perfect mold—this is true in the way we pay thousands to give our children a head start as toddlers or the way we are encouraged to choose a career path when we enter collegiate study. Such motivation to conform causes us to lose touch with what we truly want from the world by exacting universal expectations that society requires us to meet.

As much as we recognize the dangers of such prepackaged idealism, society does offer us the security that strict organization brings. Thomas Hobbes' concept of *contractarianism* suggests that we surrender many natural rights for our mutual protection from each other. In our current civilization, we not only sacrifice certain freedoms so that we can ensure that heinous acts are suppressed and punished, but submit ourselves to other requirements that extend well beyond these matters. We accept a broader social contract that entails, for instance, that we pay taxes to a higher authority to be used for economic stability and equity, and—most ironically in the context of this essay—for educational institutions. One might still say, however, that this expanded contract primarily addresses matters of security.

It is not a weakness to desire security, but we often lose sight of ourselves in our pursuit of the rules of society, and the consequences that we have discussed above have clearly become a reality in every choice we make. Thus by accepting the contract, we also accept the risk of conforming to those more subtle societal constraints. One famous case is that of Holden Caulfield of *The Catcher in the Rye*, a young man who wishes to catch children before they "fall" into the real world. He, like me, finds himself overwhelmed by the superficiality of those around him, who are so immersed in maintaining the standard that they lose their personal identity. However, unlike Holden, I am not so jaded that the world becomes so unbearable a place to inhabit. It simply becomes a place where I must be careful not to lose myself in fulfilling the expectations of others.

With such a great push for organization, we have, at times, lost ourselves in conformity and given up the chance to take risks and experience the world without outside influence. Raised in society with so many limits and boundaries, we have become trained to control our urges and to monitor our actions so that there might be a sense of safe predictability to our behavior; this can be seen at its best—or worst—in a job interview or taking an exam. Abnormality is frowned upon, and the conventional consequences of abnormality limit our potential as humans. This is disheartening to me, as it was to Holden Caulfield. There are gains to be taken in conformity, but we suffer the sacrifice of an uninfluenced, unbiased experience that we never get to touch, to smell, to taste, to see, or to feel—and *that* is a shame.

CLOSEST OF COUSINS?

Harry Kruglik

ART AND SCIENCE (WHICH, for the purposes of this paper, shall be understood to mean mathematics and the physical sciences) have a unique relationship, the recognition of which tends to elude the casual observer. Indeed, people often see art and science as polar opposites. On the one hand, science prides itself on objectivity and rigorous methods that lead to an underlying truth. On the other hand, art prides itself on subjectivity and people finding their own path to their own underlying truth. Nonetheless, science and art are cousins in that they are both manifestations of the development of human thought, and our ever-changing perception of reality.

When searching for the degree of advancement of older civilizations, there are generally two fields that an anthropologist studies—art and science. The Mayan civilization, perhaps the most advanced of its time, had highly developed astronomy and was able to erect great buildings. It is also lauded, however, for the intricacy and beauty of its paintings and jewelry. The achievements in art and science go hand in hand. I cannot think of a civilization that had remarkable achievements in one field and not the other. While a civilization may be better known for its art than its science or vice versa, there is always development of both. To learn why these enterprises go hand in hand, one must look at the producers.

Art and science are, of course, products of two different types of people, right? Everyone knows that scientists are quiet, disheveled types who wear lab coats and glasses, while artists are flamboyant and generally the opposite of scientists. This stereotype is instantly debunked by the mere mention of Leonardo da Vinci. Benjamin Franklin was a great writer; Michelangelo was a noted anatomist. Although these people are noted most for achievements in one of the fields, they demonstrated great ability in both. There is even a term for such people—the Renaissance man. Perhaps modern society pushes people to specialization, so Renaissance men (or women) aren't often seen anymore. But that's peripheral. Studies of mathematical and musical prodigies have shown that they are much alike. Many scientists played instruments as youths. Members of my own family come to mind. Architecture is a profession built on balancing science and art.

The great buildings of history are artistic and scientific marvels. The Coliseum of ancient Rome and the Sphinx and pyramids of Egypt serve as examples. More recently, the Eiffel Tower pushed science to its limits and created something beautiful. Walking around downtown Chicago, I have seen many architectural masterpieces: the Board of Trade, which is an art deco style building in the shape of a huge throne; the James Thompson Center, a steel-and-glass creation of Helmut Jahn that has a great open space inside of it that is naturally lit and extends nine stories to the roof; the Inland Steel building, clad in shiny steel; and the First Chicago Bank Building that smoothly sweeps up into the sky. These are only a few. I can think of many examples of art in or on buildings, but in these examples, the building itself is the art. Automobile manufacturers combine art and science, because they realize they must appeal to the customer's aesthetic sense as well as his or her practical sense, to sell cars. A Chevy Corvette may have a one-million horsepower engine, but it wouldn't get a second look from most people without its racy, avant-garde styling. The concept of functional art is based on combining science and art. Surely this betokens some affinity and similarity.

Having established that the development of thought in a civilization seems to manifest itself pretty well through both science and art, it is still to be determined whether or not this makes them cousins. Certainly there are many differences between them. Science involves rigorous research and experimentation and aims to make generalizations, or laws, about the environment. Mathematicians establish deductive systems within which they can have complete certainty. Art has no laws and makes no claims to certainty. Yet while it is more subjective than science, art isn't necessarily as subjective as scientists might say it is. After all, there is wide agreement that whatever art is, the works of Beethoven, Shakespeare and Michelangelo, to name a few, epitomize it. Another similarity lies in Thomas Kuhn's theories about the evolution of science, which can also be applied to art: The shift from two-dimensional paintings to paintings with depth can be seen as a paradigm shift. As painting has evolved, it has become a greater mirror of reality—the addition of depth, perspective, the sense of capturing a moment in time all represented shifts in how painting was done. When these new techniques developed, the old methods gradually fell into disuse, as with any paradigm shift.

Fashion fits into the paradigm shift model of science very well. Designers look back a hundred years and say "I don't know how people wore such ugly clothes," much like scientists, I'm sure, look back and say, "I don't know how they believed in phlogiston." Both statements of incredulity are made because a paradigm shift has occurred, and what was sensible under the old paradigm now seems strange and foreign. A man with the huge, puffy hair of Descartes would today be as out of place as one that believed planetary orbits were circular.

In the face of these similarities, scientists may still say that they are better because science is headed toward a perfect understanding of nature, while art is not. A sensible theory, which I don't necessarily endorse, counters this claim of convergence to truth in a powerful way (and in a sense quite distinct from Kuhn). "Pessimistic meta-induction from past falsity," which I would have named differently, simply says that since all previous theories of science have been proven wrong, the current ones will be, too. Even the great Einstein was wrong on some things. Science does appear to move towards greater understanding, but I would wager that art does, too. The famous hand of God reaching out to Adam in a moment in time has more power than previous art with no sense of time. Manet's *A Bar at the Folies-Bergère* is an impressionist masterpiece that conveys an understanding of humanity at many different levels. Beethoven, with his almost mathematical sense of musical logic and dynamic variation certainly had deep understanding of some kind of truth, perhaps aesthetic. There is definitely advancement there; there is a progression towards something.

Whether in the domain of physical reality, mathematical systems, or in humanity in general, both art and science are engaged in a search for truth. Practitioners of both pull their societies along and determine their level of civilization. The development of both of them by their practitioners is intuitive, even subconscious, as Henri Poincaré said about mathematical creation, and therefore mysterious. So, despite methodological and other differences, art and science truly are the closest of cousins. Maybe even brothers.

THE DEFENSE OF IVAN ILYCH

Joe Clark

IVAN ILYCH WAS A good man, whose choice of profession, and style of life, were largely noble, and carried out as they were to the benefit of society.

While Tolstoy might argue that Ilych's actions, first as a lawyer, and then as a judge ascending through the echelons of Russian well-to-do society, are fundamentally inauthentic, I assert that one should not be condemned solely on the grounds of relative personal authenticity, or lack thereof, in one's life. While he lived, Ilych's actions were honest and just, serving as they did to further the common good and to keep the courts' ponderous wheels turning in a manner consistent with the best ideals of the administration of legal systems. Parties to suits brought under the aegis of Ilych's able adjudicative powers could rest assured of a fair trial, with an equitable and reasonable resolution.

What's more, Ilych's proven juridical capacity was motivated in large part by material considerations, for he reasoned that the able execution of his office would lead to advancement, which in turn would lead to the betterment of his, and his family's, social status. But, while Tolstoy condemns and kills Ilych for this alleged inauthenticity, I contend that there is, *primae impresionis*, nothing wrong with such a situation. After all, society benefits by retaining and promoting an able bureaucrat, and the individual reaps the rewards of his actions. Resulting from this symbiotic exchange is a society primed to reward energetic and useful individuals, who are ready to act on its behalf. Capitalism generally, and the Constitutional structure of the United States in particular, is predicated on such a notion: individual ambitions compel societal members to act, and these ambitions, when channeled through an appropriately constructed governmental structure, serve the common good and propel the community forward. To this end, the Federalist Papers speak brilliantly, as does the Declaration of Independence. We are empowered to pursue life, liberty, and happiness (or, in the case of John Locke, property); the motivation of that pursuit may often be propelled by ambition. Whether that ambition emanates from within the person (what Tolstoy might term an authentic exercise of choice), or whether that ambition is a product of the culture in which we live (think *tabula rasa*), makes little difference.

Indeed, we are creatures of the society in which we live and, as such, are expected to function within its constructs and structures. Accordingly, our goals and expectations are influenced and shaped by the context of our existence; that which we value, both the material and immaterial, can (and should) be determined, at least in part, by the culture that surrounds us. Our actions, whether properly authentic or not (in the sense that Tolstoy defines those terms), are best carried out within the confines, and for the betterment, of the cultures and civilizations of which we form a part.

Take, for example, Jane Austen's *Sense and Sensibility*. Depicting two sisters, the novel pits authentic action against its inauthentic cousin. Throughout the better part of the narrative, one of the book's sisters lives on impulses that are very Tolstoy-esqe, based as they are on the preeminence of action grounded in personal desire—society and its dangerous influencing tentacles be damned! The other, however, operates within the confines of the culture's constructs, ever mindful of proper action, defined in large part by prevailing social norms. While the former sister is motivated from within, the latter is a creature acting under largely external influences.

At the end of the day, Austen sends a clear message as to which form of action she prefers, and her signal does not necessarily comport with Tolstoy's message. Her view on this matter is represented by the resolution of the two sisters' particularly vexing love lives, and Austen makes amply clear that action is best confined to societal constructs: after pursuing the love of her life, against the better judgment and traditions of her society, the "authentic" sister nearly dies from her unbridled, driven-from-within passions and goals. In contrast, the sister whose life is governed by propriety and conventionality—or perhaps by honor and discipline—ends up happily married to her preferred companion.

Of course, there must be some happy detente between operating as a brainless automaton (entirely formed by society) and living as an individual. To this end, an Odyssean degree of moderation is in order, where personal truth is balanced against the exigencies of civic life. Perhaps, in some sense, Ilych failed in the end because, in the execution of his ambition, he withdrew completely from that most personal, spiritual, and authentic of the human condition's qualities—that of love. The cold war between the two halves of his personality—the material and the metaphysical—resulted in the complete and total victory of what existentialists would later call inauthentic action: Ilych abandoned as useless and a nuisance his wife and family, preferring instead to find total and complete solace through his work. Austen's sensible sister found a reasonable balance between the two, and in the end lived happily as a result; while operating within the confines of society, allowing the outcome of her goals to be determined by its strictures, she remained personally committed to her love.

ME VS. MYSELF VS. GOD

El Clandestino

THE TIME HAS COME for me to take off my boxing gloves; it is time for me to engage in a bare-knuckled fight with myself. There will be no referee, there will be no audience, there will be no popcorn buckets—it will just be me, myself, and God. On the second day of class I was asked whether or not I believe in a God, and I coolly responded: "In my mind, I feel that God does not exist, but in my heart I feel that God must exist." However true this response is for me, it does not dig deep enough; I want to know explicitly how I feel about God and religion. By first breaking down my rationale and feelings about why the agnostic side of me cannot believe that a God exists, and then contrasting these thoughts against my deep-rooted passion for Judaism and the belief that there is a God, I will seek to understand further what my true beliefs concerning God are. Let the boxing match begin.

Round One, agnostic El Clandestino *comes out swinging hard*. I feel that it is one-hundred-percent human nature to construct the idea of God because the notion of a supreme being answers all of the festering questions that humans face, and consequently it can provide us with a great deal of comfort. After all, is it not our capacity for rational thought—to question, to seek answers, to understand causes and effects—that separates us from animals? Why would someone take the time to write the book of *Genesis*? Arguably, by nature we suffer from some generalized form of xenophobia—afraid of what we do not know—so we create God to answer all of the otherwise inexplicable questions. To illustrate this point, let us consider the Aztecs and their polytheism. According to the Aztec religion, if the people needed rain, they would pray to the god of rain or water. Now compare their idea of praying for rain to our modern day conception of meteorology. Today, we understand—or at least think we understand––the reasons why it rains and how to predict when it will or will not rain. The Aztecs, who did not have this scientific knowledge, had no ability to control or to plan their agriculture with respect to rainfall. I would then conjecture that they thus created the god of rain—and similarly many of their other deities—both to explain and, via prayer and ritual, to influence an element of their environment crucial to their survival. Even those of us who might deny vehemently the truth and effectiveness of such a system of beliefs and rites can still understand the sense of comfort that would likely attend the associated sense of understanding and control.

This notion of creating a God to answer the unknowns in life and to give an individual the feeling of more security is by no means limited to the Aztecs, and I would not be surprised if it applied to most religions. Just as the Aztecs created Gods to help them cope with their lives, so did the Israelites create their one God, and so forth for other religions as well. This is, of course, an enormously bold statement, especially considering how much of our world is, and how much of human history has been, dominated by religion. But does the vast spread and power of religion justify the truth of religious beliefs? I do not think so. After all, is it not true that humans today, and humans 2006 years ago, and humans 5766 years ago, all share the distinct quality of asking questions to rationalize the world's enigmas? While I cannot answer this question definitively, given that I agree with how Vercors defines what it means to be human in *You Shall Know Them*, the answer would seem to be, *yes*. Therefore humans have always had that same inquisitive, rationalizing quality and thus have always been capable of—or susceptible to—the creation of religions.

Round two, agnostic El Clandestino *continues to maul his challenger, showing no mercy.* My sense of intellectual integrity does not allow me to believe in religion because in order for me to believe in a religion, I would have to know that I believed in "the real religion" which prays to "the real God." If, in fact, a person were part of a religion that did not pray to the real God (or gods), then essentially not only would all of his or her devotion be for nothing, but it would further constitute blasphemous activity that would displease the real God. So what would enable an individual to know that he or she were praying to the real God and observing the real religion? I cannot think of a single reason which is not in itself part of a religious doctrine. For example, a Jewish person might say, "I know I am praying to the real God because God selected the Jews as the chosen people, and so therefore, since I am part of the chosen people, I must be part of the real religion and thus praying to the real God." This seems like a baseless claim to me because this kind of justification is merely the religion itself claiming its own validity. Thus I cannot believe in *any* religion because many religions claim to pray to their own distinctive real God, and there is no way for me to know which, if any, religion is the real—and consequently the true—religion.

Round three, the religious El Clandestino *looks like he is getting into his rhythm as his competitor tires from such an early full-scale assault.* Where does all this doubting and denial of God and religion leave me? Surely somewhere alongside Freud's belief that religion is merely a delusion created by man, and surely somewhere alongside an existentialist such as Sybil from the Vercors novel. But what are the consequences of me holding this belief? Am I left with the confidence of knowing that I know the truth and that I get to laugh at all the ignorant religious followers? No, not at all, because for just as I say "prove that God exists," another may respond, "prove that God does not exist." So what am I left with? Not much. It seems like all I really get out of not being a true believer is a brain full of skepticism and maybe the peace of mind that I am not buying into something which cannot be universally acknowledged as true. How do I feel when I enclose myself in this agnostic mentality? I feel that Sybil's poignant observation encapsulates my feelings quite well: "I can't get used to how meaningless it all is." But as it turns out, I am not completely against the belief of God and religion, and like I said earlier, it is just my brain, but not my heart, which takes that stance.

Round four, religious El Clandestino *looks rejuvenated and poised to gain ground.* If I am not completely against God and religion, what questions arise in my mind or heart which seem to indicate that I do believe in God and Judaism? How could it be possible that the Jews have survived for this long without any help from God? How could a group so small in number, only 0.00227 percent of the entire world population, according to jewishvirtuallibrary.org, be blessed with being so successful as to have won an astounding 21% of all Nobel Prize awards from 1901 to 2005? How could a people who have been so passionately persecuted throughout their entire history, with such colossal enemies as the Egyptians, the Romans, the Spanish in the Inquisition, the Soviets in the Pogroms, Nazi Germany in the Holocaust, and six Arab countries attacking Israel at once in its war for independence, still be around today? Is it possible that a group of people could have not only survived but also thrived for so long without the help of God?

If I do not actually believe in religion, then how is it that every single time I hear the "Hatikva" ("The Hope"), Israel's national anthem, I infallibly get goose-bumps? If I do not actually believe in religion, how is it that I am able to make myself fast for Yom Kippur (Day of Atonement)? If I do not actually believe in religion, how can it be that I feel an inexplicably powerful bond with my Jewish friends that I do not feel with my gentile friends? If I do not actually believe in religion, why is it that I carry the "Tefillat Haderech" (Traveler's Prayer) everywhere I go since I spent five safe weeks in Israel the summer of my junior year? If I do not actually believe in religion, then why do I compulsively read up on Israel-related news every day and boil over with sorrow, concern, or anger when the news is not good? If I do not actually believe in religion, why is it that people so often see me in—and that I accept—the role of being the "token Jew?" If I do not actually believe in religion, why have I attempted to pray directly to God? If I do not actually believe in religion, why would I even be debating the existence of God in this paper?

Round five, agnostic El Clandestino *is on the ropes and taking many severe blows.* Through my questioning it appears that the general themes of why I do believe in Judaism, or at least why I do not, *not* believe in Judaism, go as follows. First, I cannot comprehend how the Jewish people have been around so long without in fact being, to some extent—but by no means in an I-am-better-than-you, arrogant type of way—chosen by God. This belief presents a direct but incomplete response to the previously addressed issue of not being able to believe in religion because I could not know which religion is true. Secondly, I cannot deny the fervent passion that I feel for Jewish people and Israel. Lastly, though I cannot explain my adherence to certain religious practices, I carry them out regardless. It is also very important to note that much of my questioning does not have to do with the religion of Judaism itself, but rather the nature of my relationship with Jewish people. From this, I feel it is safe to say that I do not believe in the Judaism itself in the sense of, "I must obey all of God's commandments and in turn God will take care of me," but rather that I find great comfort and am quite passionate about Jewish culture and my Jewish identity.

Round six, the boxers continue to exchange blows, but a clear winner is far from sight. This conjecture leads me full circle back to my initial remark: "In my mind, I feel that God does not exist, but in my heart, I feel that God must exist." I can now further understand my claim by tying in my whole mental journey: to me, religion of the heart alone represents spirituality, whereas religion of the mind alone represents actual belief in the doctrines of a religion. So while I do not believe that not eating pork will make God happy and consequently I will be held in higher regard in God's mind,

I still do not eat pork because I enjoy being a part of something larger than myself and being able to relate to others through tradition in a "Fiddler on the Roof" sort of way. So after six rounds of hard-fought boxing what conclusion have I arrived at? Unfortunately, without a knockout, six rounds are not enough to come to a decision with such heavyweights in the ring. Or maybe this is not so unfortunate, after all, what fun would life be if I was able to answer one of its hardest questions before even turning twenty? Through fighting myself and my own beliefs about God and religion I have realized that just as the world is unable to prove or disprove religion as a whole, I am unable to prove or disprove where my true core beliefs reside, and consequently I must admit that I simply do not know enough to be able to arrive at a concrete conclusion. What, then, has questioning God and religion, and more generally the *Questions of Civilization* class taught me? That I know nothing with complete certainty, but that acknowledging the imperfection of my knowledge is perfectly fine.

Tự Hòi: The Question

Arun Shrestha

SUNDAY, JUNE 19, 1999 will probably remain, more than any other, as the day my life changed. No single life-altering event took place on that particular day, but rather a decision that would set me on the path I am on today. It was the day I embarked upon my journey from Manila, the place of my birth, to Dhaka, Bangladesh, a place of which I knew little at the time. My father had given me the tourist guide description of the nation, characterizing Dhaka as the bustling city that was torn between its turbulent past and promising future. Little did I know that that equated to a very uncertain present.

Upon landing under the cloak of night, I was whisked away to a hotel at the heart of Dhaka, unaware of the situation around me. It had been a long day and I was happy to be ignorant of my surroundings. It was only the next morning when I got a stern wake up call, and not one from the concierge. I drew open the curtains and was greeted by Dhaka, *au naturel*. Never in my life had the sun provided me with so much light. I peered out of the window and into the streets, my eyes widening by the second. It was too much for just one glance. At first it seemed like an Andy Warhol image, just a blur of colors. As my eyes focused in, I found a maze of streets congested with rickshaws, three wheelers and dilapidated old busses filled to the brim with commuters. People were everywhere: on the streets, sidewalks, bus and van roofs and even jammed into the road dividers. It was as if Dhaka was in a perpetual state of pandemonium, much like a boy band concert, only worse. This to me really brought to life the statistic that Dhaka was the most densely populated city on earth.

It was when I fully realized this that the bomb dropped. It was then that I began to comprehend all of the luxuries I had given up in coming to Dhaka and started to seriously doubt whether the decision to move was the right one. Still trying to take in all of what I saw, I sat myself down on the bed. For the first time in my life, I was truly overwhelmed. I was still reeling from the effects of the view from the window as I ventured out house hunting with my parents. What struck me was that whenever the traffic was stagnant, one, or sometimes two, or even three beggars would approach the car, asking for money. But the state of the beggars was unlike anything else I had ever seen. Living my sheltered and shamefully oblivious life in Manila had protected me from such horrible scenes. But in Dhaka, it was inescapable. Mutilation was everywhere. The congestion of the city I could handle, but the mutilation was something quite different: people without arms, legs and limbs just desperately and aimlessly walking about the streets, begging for a mere Taka, equivalent to one-fiftieth of a U.S. Dollar. The state of desperation was something my mind was unable to comprehend.

As time went on, I realized that the handicapped weren't the only people who suffered under these cruel conditions. Old women who, after a long life of hard work, deserved to be cherished by family in the comfort of a house were instead ridiculed on the streets. Children, robbed of their youth and education, seemed jaded at the tender age of eight or so. Disease ravaged people of all ages, who belonged in hospital beds, yet instead made the footpaths and streets their home. This was the uncertain state of modern Dhaka. Seeing suffering of this magnitude creates a permanent imprint in one's mind, and certainly forces things into perspective.

When first arriving in Dhaka, it seemed like it would be impossible to ignore the plight of these unfortunate people, and I couldn't understand the apparent cruelty of the local population who looked upon these scenes with much complacency. However, as time passed, I, too, grew in complacency and realized that Shakespeare was indeed right; familiarity does breed contempt. As the years went by, hard as it was and impossible as it seemed, I was able to tune out some of the suffering around me, though I wondered at times whether it was the right thing to do. I brushed the thought aside in favor of more cheerful and less controversial topics and diversions.

But as the time neared to leave Bangladesh, on one of those many sleepless nights, the people of the streets reentered my mind, as if to teach me one last lesson before leaving their country. I thought of all the poverty I had seen on my trips into the countryside, and on my community service trips within Dhaka. I realized that I was taking the easy way out by plunging myself into a comfortable oblivion rather than trying to better the lives of these impoverished people. I had had the privilege to see what I had seen, and now I had the power to rectify some of the inequities of which I had now become aware. As the plane sped down the drenched runway a couple minutes past midnight on August 12, I kept this in mind and vowed that these people's suffering would not be in vain. As the Airbus quietly took to the skies, as I saw the clouds and the stars near and knew that I was taking off for the last time from my home of three years—a home I had come to love—I remembered the men, women and children of the streets of Dhaka less as beggars and more as teachers. They had instilled within me a value that I shall carry with me for the rest of my life.

When reading Graham Greene's *The Quiet American*, much of what I had felt during my early and last days in Dhaka came rushing back. As the novel continued, I was progressively taken back in time, and once again experienced the raw emotion that I had felt so often while living in Bangladesh. One thing, however, was different: The re-ignited feelings sparked by Greene's novel returned with a renewed intensity. Yet it seemed to me that with the benefit of hindsight, two subsequent years in Manila, and all that has happened in the interim between then and now, my vow to do something about the abject poverty had dissolved into an occasional thought. As I read through *The Quiet American*, I became more and more disappointed and enraged at myself for having done so. I felt the burning urge to try to explain my true feelings about the massive disparity that separate the two worlds that co-exist today; the material one where one finds depth in appearances, the other, one of a very harsh reality and difficulty, where getting through one night alive is considered a success. Having realized the plight of one of the most impoverished peoples on earth, yet re-immersing myself in the material world upon my return to Manila was an act I deemed inexcusable. Harshly brought back to my senses by *The Quiet American*, I once again felt the grave necessity to do something about it. First, however, I needed to get across what I felt was my tumultuous journey between the two worlds, and where I find myself now, hopefully removed from either world, wary of being completely sucked into either. My thoughts came to rest in conjunction with Buddha's in the form of the middle path; the extremes of either world would be inferior; to balance between the two, acknowledging, realizing and experiencing in small quantities both worlds would be optimal. The first step towards achieving that sacred balance would be to put forth what I feel, with all my experiences behind me. The end result is this poem.

Truthfully, I don't know how this novel sparked all these feelings within me once again. Call it the Asian connection: I feel an affinity with most things Asian, especially in literature, history and politics. I have lived in the third world for my entire life, and contrary to what most people may think upon hearing that, I consider it a blessing to have done so. It has exposed me to so many aspects of life that I would have avoided had I lived only in the developed world. It has provided an excellent juxtaposition of circumstances—of affluence and poverty—and hence a rich base from which to view life. This amalgamation of unique and diverse experiences has grounded me on several levels and made me a more aware person, and I consider myself so very lucky for having gone through them.

Tự Hỏi

Waves of reality
Lifting me unexpectedly
Looking inside to see
Visions of poverty

Ego lies in human nature
Scars the face in every one of us
Almost as if to lose the faith we ignore
What's mine is mine
What's yours is yours

It is this that
Sets a wider gap between us
We build walls without shame
We turn away
If you're not one of us
Though there's only one color in our blood

But like the north needs the south
The wind needs the clouds
To all these reasons of life
We need them
More than they need us

Another day goes by
Another moon
Another sun
Time spent reminiscing on events past
Only to the torment of their souls
As it is passion they've lived without

We, however voluntarily and inexcusably
Live in complete oblivion
As greed demands our full attention
We only live for our own gain it seems

At times, however
For but an ephemeral moment
I sit in realization
On this place we call earth
So filled with
Death and despair
Suffering and sorrow
Yet I close
My eyes
My ears
My mind
And am lifted to
Where the wind dances
To the song of the birds
Where the flowers
Sway gently to the rhythm of the wind
As I gaze into this world
I see something
Its purity
Undeniable
Its innocence and naivety
Beyond dispute
Its equality
Beautiful

If for that one evanescent moment
Realization was complete
Why not carry it on for an eternity?

Tự Hỏi: The Question

I've flown through oceans for clarity
To comprehend more about you and me
I've witnessed joy, I've witnessed misery
Yet
I've seen richness, I've seen poverty

As we pursue living a life that's so superficial
And as they continue to drown in their own tears of sorrow
To realize their plight
Yet to do nothing...
To rise above this
Or to be immersed into it...
For an eternity of transient lifetimes
That truly is the question.

THE MASTER AT CMC

Cameron Hanson

LEADERSHIP COMES IN MANY forms; it varies for each culture and time period. With leadership comes much burden and responsibility. While both Confucius and Claremont McKenna College support high qualifications for leadership, their vision, skills, and values with respect to how students should guide society are often conflicting. The main difference is the root of their pursuits. Through *The Analects*, Confucius preaches a collective approach in which every individual's goal is for the good of society and one's family. In contrast, CMC teaches individualism: each of us is responsible by means of our many virtues and intense efforts to achieve understanding of our surroundings and then to use this knowledge for the benefit of others. Within CMC, a primary goal is success in one's professional field, often measured by accumulated wealth. My personal beliefs lie between those of Confucius and

CMC. I relate to the more modern perspectives of CMC in which my hard work and perseverance will bring me closer to my goal, though my Catholic religion and the morals with which I have been raised encourage me to value the Confucian ideals of reciprocity and gratitude. For this reason, much of my spiritual and intrinsic motivations can be seen in the idealistic preachings of Confucius, but my practical striving for success and ability to make a difference in my society is rooted in the CMC philosophy.

The ultimate goal of Confucius is to achieve overarching harmony within family and society. In addition, the core of his code of ethics embodies many other values that Confucius feels should govern daily life. He stresses humility by teaching that family and elders (anyone wiser or above oneself) deserve obedience, respect, loyalty, and fair treatment. One should live moderately, and not indulge in irrelevant activities that distract oneself from *Tao*, his very real way and path to humaneness and virtue. Even the choice of one's diet is significant: Confucius advises simplicity in the consumption of food. Self-discipline is foremost, as well as ritual and reverence to the divine. Through this base of morals, Confucius idealizes how leaders should use their talents.

CMC expects good citizenship from its students, with the ultimate goal to prepare bright young men and women, who have been challenged in all ways of thinking and living, to face the real world with strong knowledge and an open mind. With that said, CMC does not just cultivate students with the sole intent of personal success; rather, they strive to foster an environment that encourages recreation, cultural diversity, and respect and camaraderie for all. CMC, as a secular and politically correct institution, does not impose a standard of religious belief, but does offer religious courses to enlighten our minds and spirit.

My personal set of values combines the teachings of Confucius with those of CMC. I put family above all, and my main concern is to love and to protect them. Likewise, Confucius places respect and honor of one's family as paramount, though he would probably argue that equal service to both family and society should bring harmony, while I would probably choose family over society in a desperate situation, were the two ever to fall into conflict. As Confucius revered his ancestry, I strongly value my faith and the belief in the wonder of God and His ability to guide me throughout my life. And more in line with the values of CMC, the opportunity to learn and grow intellectually is extremely important to me. Next, I value empathy as well as reciprocity and gratitude. I have so much to be thankful for, that I must give back and show compassion to others, just as Confucius teaches. Finally, I feel that each individual should have the right to better one's life as well as those around them, and that the personal pursuit of happiness is inherent in every human being. CMC would argue that each individual has this ability of personal fulfillment, while Confucius gives priority to collective success. I therefore fall somewhere between Confucius and CMC largely as a result of current social values and the fact that CMC does not, as an institution, emphasize personal morals and spiritual values, which Confucianism does.

Both *The Analects* and CMC—and I, too—have different approaches to how we as students should lead society. Confucius argues that we should be obedient to our elders, and that all of our actions should subsequently serve the higher good of bettering our society. Confucius does not think that "the gentleman's training should be confined to particular skills so that he may become the tool or implement of others." Instead, "it must develop his moral qualities and powers of leadership." Just as at CMC, the qualities of a leader are very important, but Confucius desires a man who will make adherence to established precepts his primary goal, someone who will exemplify the pious qualities of a gentleman. "If one is loyal and faithful in word and sincere and respectful in deed, then even in barbarian countries one will make progress." Via the Confucian values of humility and reverence, there is much less conflict and competition than in today's modern society. The United States's free market and democratic formation do not support the Confucian idea of communal peace. In the Master's words, he prefers governance by "non-action." This theory of harmony without conflict goes directly against CMC's teaching of laissez-faire economics and the idea that with hard work and smart maneuvering, anyone can rise to the top in business. Thus Confucius considers education an important element of society, but only insofar as it is directed toward the attainment of knowledge of culture and propriety. Both at CMC and in my own previous experiences, education is about not only learning the facts to a math problem or book in literature, but discussing and arguing all topics that influence and hence *change* society, from the Napoleonic wars, to the death penalty, to one's own personal values. Moreover, at the core of modern education is the emphasis on experiencing as much of the world as possible, even if some of these experiences are negative, because collectively they add to the broadening of one's mind. Again, the differences come down to how each side defines its goals. The Master preaches that every member of society must work towards harmony as a collective whole; CMC gives every individual the opportunity to reach any level in one's personal and professional life.

My practical goals follow the vision of CMC, while my aspirations within the social aspect of my life adhere more to the teachings of Confucius. I want what most other people of the modern world desire, the American dream: monetary and emotional success through reaching my professional potential, as well as surrounding myself with people and material luxuries (nice home, nice clothes, the good fortune of traveling) that make me feel happy. In addition to these indulgences that Confucius would certainly not condone, I strive to continue and strengthen my ongoing relationship with God, and constantly to be aware of my duty to treat others with consideration and gratitude. I feel that relationships with others are one of the most essential parts of our existence, and proper respect and appreciation to all those in my life are a must. Therefore, I combine the values of *The Analects* and CMC to define my future pursuits as I begin to take on the responsibility of leading my society as a young and educated woman.

Values are subjective to each individual and custom, and thus it is inevitable that there are great differences between the teachings of Confucius and CMC. Nonetheless, many of the ancient Chinese values transcend time and place, including humility, respect, reciprocity, and spiritual ritual. CMC's values are simply the practical application of all of our abilities in the real world. What remains are the different perspectives of collectivism versus individualism. There is no right or wrong way of living, and each of us must choose among values from all genres to create our own personal code of conduct.

IMAGES OF SOCRATES: TRUTH OR PERSPECTIVE?

Allison Strother

SOCRATES, A LEGENDARY GREEK philosopher, generated much controversy during his time, and this controversy continues to this day. It is therefore unsurprising that authors portray Socrates in very different fashions. Aristophanes, a renowned Greek playwright, mocks Socrates by painting him as a frivolous, fraudulent fool in the play *Clouds*, while Plato, another Greek philosopher, depicts Socrates as a virtuous man wrongly accused of several crimes in his *Apology of Socrates*. Whether one or the other is indeed correct in his portrayal is, of course, subject to debate.

To Aristophanes, Socrates, a ridiculous rogue who dupes his pupils and teaches dishonorable speech methods, has a very negative influence on society. The main character of *Clouds*, a man named Strepsiades, pays Socrates to learn how to avoid his creditors through Socrates' famed "unjust speech," a notion later personified in the play. Unfortunately for Strepsiades, his plan backfires in two ways. First, senility prevents him from mastering this manner of speech. Second, his son, after later learning from Unjust Speech, uses his new knowledge to rationalize beating his father (Strepsiades) and his mother. Clearly Aristophanes sees Socrates as a dangerous influence that poisons the minds of those under his tutelage. By allowing Strepsiades' son to learn a method of speech that enables him to justify abusing his parents, Socrates flouts a fundamental Greek principle: respect for one's elders. Unjust Speech not only encompasses disrespect for elders, it also exhorts one to "believe that nothing is shameful," decries moderation, and reveals that "the public advocates...tragedians...[and] the popular orators" all come from the "buggered," a group of those who are either passive homosexuals or who are punished in the same manner as the homosexuals. Essentially, Unjust Speech encourages one to break with almost every major convention of Greek society, an extremely pernicious teaching which, in Aristophanes' mind (as argued by Just Speech, the antithesis of Unjust Speech) should be eradicated since it erodes conventional Greek values. Socrates moreover claims that "Zeus doesn't even exist," and purports that the only gods are the Clouds, Wind and the tongue. Challenging the existence of traditional Greek gods, especially Zeus, is tantamount to treason, as this blasphemy completely contradicts mainstream Greek teaching. Thus, Socrates' unbelief again illustrates Aristophanes' view of Socrates as a detrimental influence on Athenian society.

In contrast, Plato, as seen in his *Apology of Socrates*, views Socrates as a wise man who unfortunately becomes a scapegoat because his speeches condemn the self-righteousness of many prominent Athenians. According to Socrates himself, "the god in Delphi" tells a man named Chaerephon that "no one was wiser" than Socrates; in his disbelief, Socrates travels around investigating and trying to ascertain the truth of this oracle. Finding that his wisdom lies in the fact that he is cognizant of his own ignorance, Socrates realizes that he does possess more wisdom than anyone else, for others all believe that they have wisdom when in actuality they do not. In Socrates' mind, this gives him a divine mandate to highlight others' erroneous opinions of themselves, and in doing so he incurs much hatred. Thus, Socrates' self-defense rests on this claim. As to the accusations brought against him, such as corruption of youth and knowledge of unjust speech, Socrates asserts that they have no factual basis; he invites witnesses or anyone with proof of his wrongdoing to speak out, but none do so. Plato portrays Socrates as a completely rational man who has not only committed no crime, but has benefited Athenian society by reminding them of their folly. To Plato, Socrates' devotion to this pursuit is laudable, especially in the face of those who wish him ill.

It is difficult to say which of the two portrayals of Socrates is correct since both views can be somewhat reconciled. For instance, though Socrates may be "corrupting" the Athenian youth in the sense that he questions their elders and points out their flaws, he also teaches them to think critically rather than automatically acquiescing to the opinions of their elders. From an elder's perspective, this may constitute corruption, but such corruption allows the new generation of young people to broaden their thinking and, most importantly, think for themselves. This ultimately confers more benefit to society.

Furthermore, Socrates' "unjust speech" teaches that men who make an impact on society do not conform to societal customs; in fact, it is because they break with these customs that they profoundly influence society. Though this upsets the order and serenity of Athens, it contributes to the city's prosperity in the long run. Without men who present novel ideas, radical though they may be, a society stagnates and cannot progress. Change is wrought by those who dare to challenge convention, not by those who continue in the "just" traditional ways of society. Consequently, a more appropriate term for Socrates' "unjust speech" might be "practical speech."

The same idea applies to Socrates' disregard for Zeus in the Aristophanes play and by implication, for the other traditional Greek gods. Aristophanes intends for this unbelief to illustrate Socrates' foolishness; this "foolishness," however, confirms Socrates' independence. He does not acquiesce to society's insistence upon convention, but instead defies conformity and unashamedly pursues his own unpopular ideas.

Plato's Socrates seems to me the more "ethical" or "moral" Socrates.

He tirelessly toils, without any compensation or reward for his work, to reveal the misguided opinions men have of themselves and about their world. This Socrates believes his course of action demonstrates the utmost virtue and morality, and he frequently invokes the idea that his mission comes from a god. Plato's Socrates also understands the difficulties of living morally among those who do not; this is evidenced by his repeated explanations of why he accomplishes much of his work privately. In Aristophanes, in contrast, Socrates lives as a profligate in a supposedly otherwise moral and ethical society. This Socrates makes no claims with respect to ethics. Rather, he appears somewhat unconcerned with the state of the world around him and spends his days sequestered in his "thinkery." Morals have no bearing in Socrates' world. To him, pondering and contemplating constitute worthy-enough pursuits.

I cannot say which image of Socrates is more correct. Both portrayals have their merits and faults. Aristophanes' Socrates (and his allied character Unjust Speech) thinks more practically about the world, but Plato's Socrates lives more nobly because he deliberately pursues his concept of morality, even to his own disadvantage. While others may see the idealistic perspective as more appealing than the pragmatic one, I believe that taking a pragmatic view of the world ultimately leads to less disappointment and to a more accurate evaluation of people and situations. As a result, I am more disposed toward Aristophanes' Socrates, though I do not believe that his is the more correct characterization. Ideally, I would like to agree with Plato's Socrates, but unfortunately, the state of the world and human nature prevents me from doing so.

WHAT DEFINES A GOOD PERSON?

Alison Ryan

ONE QUESTION ASKED BY man for centuries is "What does it mean to be a good person?" No two people on the planet identically define the term "good person" and even two people with infinitesimal differences in their definitions may choose to follow their guidelines for moral behavior differently. This, the essential question of morality, is relevant because it affects the conduct of our society on every level. Religion, of course, strongly influences how many people define a good person because religious indoctrination often fuses one's view of goodness with his or her deity's view. In my personal experience, my definition of a good person has been most strongly affected not by religion, but rather by the progression of my own morals as I continue to grow and to define my personal beliefs via exposure to different schools of thought.

I believe that a good person attempts to better herself through the acquisition of knowledge and the examination of the world around her. I share Socrates' belief that "the unexamined life is not worth living," and that a person who does not question and explore the world around her does not fit the definition of a good person. It is important to question all aspects of our lives, especially our leaders and our beliefs, in order to maintain independent thought. I do not feel that the definition of a good person should be defined solely by religious doctrine because this discourages independent thought and causes people to act righteously for the wrong reasons, reasons such as fear of eternal damnation. I believe that a good person encompasses the idea of "do good and disappear" in her daily routine and other activities, although failure to do so does not necessarily constitute a "bad person." To "do good and disappear" instead of attempting to be recognized for good deeds makes one's actions more noble; it demonstrates modesty, one of the essential components of goodness. Although a boastful person can be moral and giving, desiring credit and recognition for good deeds and moral behavior detracts greatly from one's stature as a good person.

A good person should be driven by internal forces to better herself and others rather than by any external factors. As stated in the *Bhagavad-Gita*, "Don't be concerned with the fruits of your actions; act justly and for the sake of it." Although some would argue that a good person aims to appear noble in the eyes of others, I believe that one should be driven by one's inner sense of goodness to act nobly and righteously. Ivan Ilych in *The Death of Ivan Ilych*, by Leo Tolstoy, lacked this authenticity; all of his goals came from purely extrinsic considerations, such as his desire for a high-ranking job and the acquisition of material goods. Although Ivan lived richly in the material sense, he was, at heart, detached from the world and was poor in the emotional sense. In contrast, Ivan's servant Gerasim exemplifies all that a good person should be because his goodness is internally driven; his simple and direct compassion and way of living finally force Ivan Ilych to question his entire manner of existence. Gerasim also exemplifies the idea of "do good and disappear" because he is not entitled to serve as Ivan Ilych's sick nurse and does not receive any true recognition for his efforts, but he serves Ivan just the same. These actions support the universal definition of a good person as one who acts because of the goodness in his or her heart, not because of extravagant rewards. As stated in the Bible, "The Lord seeth not as a man seeth; for man looketh on the outward appearance, but the Lord looketh on the heart." (I Samuel, 16:7) Although I do not believe in God, this quote makes an extremely vital argument about the makeup of a good person. One who boasts about her good deeds and accomplishments is likely to appear to others as a better person than one who does not publicize her works, which thereby remain largely unknown to others. However, as the biblical verse explains, exteriors matter very little. What is instead truly important is that one knows—or, for religious individuals, that God knows—that she is a good person whose morals and positive actions benefit society.

Ivan Ilych's motivation by the external forces of convention is comparable to acting morally in order to get into heaven, rather than in consequence of one's self-respect and internal goodwill. The Christian definition of a good person is one who adheres fully to the Ten Commandments and follows the Word as closely as possible. If one sins or otherwise strays from the Word of God, it is still possible to gain entry into Heaven, but repentance is necessary. I agree with much of the world, that the Ten Commandments indeed encourage moral behavior that leads to one being good; yet I do not believe straying from these commandments makes one a "bad person" or damned to burn in eternal hellfire. I believe that religion should be used constructively to define principles of morality, rather than being used to scare people into behaving themselves. Freud theorizes in *Civilization and Its Discontents* that guilt is one of the central problems threatening our civilization. This theory ties into the idea of religion causing guilt which in turn encourages people to behave morally to avoid this negative sentiment. A certain degree of guilt is healthy because it encourages positive behavior, but I believe that a truly good person does not act nobly out of guilt but rather is inspired by the goodness that lies within.

Freud, I think, would wholeheartedly object to the biblical definition of a good person. For example, again in *Civilization and Its Discontents*, he objects to the idea of "love thy neighbor" in part because his personal belief is that our primal instinct is to exhibit aggression against our fellow man rather than to express love towards one another, especially outside of the bonds of kinship. I do not hold a Freudian view in terms of the goodness of mankind. I believe that men are inherently good and that "loving thy neighbor" or, in other words, showing respect, compassion, and kindness towards our fellow man, is a large part of what defines a good person. In a somewhat different connection, Freud also asserts that "virtue [often] forfeits some part of its promised reward," by which he means that the more virtuously we behave (driven by the internally directed aggressions of the superego), the less we derive peace and happiness from our good acts. While I believe that to a certain extent Freud is correct, I nonetheless feel that in general virtuous beings reap more rewards than those without virtue. Overall, Freud might even argue that a truly good person does not exist—a view that clashes with my own.

Before coming to Claremont McKenna College, I honestly had never directly asked myself what it means to be a good person, although I have always attempted to act based on my own idea of righteous behavior. Never had I considered this question from a philosophical point of view; I had examined it simply from a moralistic perspective. My morals included the beliefs that stealing is wrong, lying is wrong under most circumstances, one should treat others as they wish to be treated, and humans should help others in need. Upon reflecting on past behavior, I realized that like many other humans, I altered my definition of a good person upon immoral behavior in order to ease my guilty conscience. These actions accord with Freud's belief in the powerful agency of guilt. If everyone tries to warp his or her definition of goodness in order to compensate for poor behavior, society will face a multitude of moral problems.

Next semester, I will enroll in an introductory class which explores Asian religions and I believe that the material presented in this course will impact my definition of a good person. As a young adult who has been raised solely in the Southern United States, the image of a good person with which I have been presented is largely Anglo-Saxon and biblical in nature. This class will present me with an eastern approach to ethics which is likely to further mold my view. My father, in fact, exemplifies this shift from a western to eastern definition of a good person. He was raised in the Catholic Church but left the church in order to practice Buddhism. Buddhism defines a good person as a good child for parents, a good student for teachers, a good friend for friends, a good member of the community, and a good employee for employers. I fully concur with this view. I believe a good person's moral standing is largely based on her interactions with others. Already through my personal exploration of Buddhism I have begun to change my morals and therefore my definition of a good person. I see now that not only does a good person behave morally, but she attempts to break the cycle of dissatisfaction in her life and chooses the optimistic view of life that all things must pass. As I explore other Asian religions and continue my studies, it is likely that my view of a good person will continue to change substantially.

Although there will never be a definition of a good person that is set in stone, there are many overlapping characteristics that can be found in literary works, religious doctrines, and cultures that contribute to a general, even universal definition. A good person can be generally defined as one who attempts to better himself, is driven by his internal desire to achieve great things, and does not boast about his achievements. As we grow, learn, and expand our horizons, our definition of a good person grows with us. Already during my short eighteen years my definition of a good person has changed significantly, and I looked forward to shaping this definition as I gain more knowledge about the world, and experience all that life has to offer.

What Is the Meaning of Life?

Shayna Williams

OF ALL OF THE topics we have examined this semester in class, the one that has affected me the most in these months is the question of the meaning of life. I don't mean the question of the reason for or the purpose of life on earth as a biophysical phenomenon, down to the single-celled organism—rather I want to address the meaning of *my* life, or of any *one* human life. I want to know why we have this brief existence and what we should do with it since we have it. My difficulty with this question is that while there are reasons to believe that there is a meaning of life that exists independently of human beings, there is also reason to believe that individuals create or invent meaning merely as a way to make life livable while they go through the instinctive biochemical processes that lead to the perpetuation of the species. More than that, it seems to me that ultimately people choose their own meaning of life based on what they want—*which means that there is no universal meaning of life separate from the individual.* So if meaning would simply cease to exist without constantly changing people constantly redefining it, how is it that it *means* anything at all? All of that aside, in all honesty I just prefer to believe that the meaning of life that I have chosen for myself is equally as correct, albeit arbitrary, as the meanings to which others cling.

Before this class I had considered the question of the meaning of life (or at least the meaning of my life), but I hadn't considered it to be of philosophical importance. I thought that the meaning of life was merely an aspect of the question of what happens to people after they die. When I was a Christian, I *knew* without a doubt that the meaning of life was to serve God and to live in such a way as to get into heaven; but when I stopped believing in God or an afterlife I stopped considering that there was any meaning of life at all. It seemed to me that if there is no higher power that created life, then there cannot be a purpose to life. Rather, the existence of any one human being must be the result of random chance and evolutionary trends; and in that case there certainly could not be a standard meaning of life that is applicable to every individual. Having considered all of this, by the time I sat down in my chair on the first day of class, I had already adopted a very existentialist view of the world, and especially of the meaning of life. In fact, the theme of my first essay was that I didn't believe that there was any one meaning of life and that I didn't think it mattered what a person chose for her personal purpose.

As the semester continued, however, the assigned readings and class discussions led me to question my existentialist viewpoint. It seems like the topics were presented in order to chip off layers of my wall of calm confidence one by one. The discussion that first made a dent in my wall was the topic of why we CMC students as a whole choose to put extensive time and effort into overachieving. While the correlated texts of *The Analects of Confucius* and the *Tao Te Ching* did not shake my foundation or prove to influence me very much, I remember that I sat in class writing down notes about why my self-imposed stress about school and grades could be justified by the promise of future success and stability. Not long after we finished the East Asian texts, we discussed Freud and whether my classmates and I, as hardworking college students, are merely living up to some expectation of our parents, or some other authoritative institution, rather than actually pursuing our own goals. I was adamantly confident that I had chosen this path on my own, and that it was precisely what satisfied my idea of who I want to be. But then I realized that a large part of the reason I am who I am is because I try to be just the *opposite* of the authorities in my life that have hurt me in the past—so in a way the meaning of life I have chosen for myself is even less my own than it would be if I had gladly accepted the guidance offered to me. Now the dent in the wall of my confidence in my purpose was getting bigger.

The most influential text in shaking my ideas and eventually knocking down the metaphorical wall I had built was Tolstoy's *The Death of Ivan Ilych*. Ivan Ilych lived a life that can be easily compared to mine. Our circumstances differ greatly, but our goals are very similar. In the same way that before his sickness Ivan lived a life of propriety and success derived from hard work and distancing himself from obstructions, I am working hard and aiming for a life that is accepted by society to be good in every way. Already, I have so removed myself from my family and my home state that I only talk to my relatives once a month; and (including this summer) I will only see them for four weeks out of the twelve months since I left home last August. The story of Ivan Ilych led me to think morbidly about how I would feel if I was suddenly diagnosed with terminal cancer. Would I be happy with the short life I have lived? Would I want to continue school and hard work in order to move toward a goal I would never reach? I decided that I would want to drop out of CMC and go back home to Oklahoma to spend my final months or years with my family. Still, I am not dying so quickly, so I continue to ignore the people I love in the interest of far-off goals that I may never reach—goals that are so influential in my life that I follow them wholeheartedly without even really understanding why I have chosen them. In short, this class has made me think that maybe the meaning of life that I have chosen for myself is pointless, and maybe even detrimental to my happiness.

In an attempt to find another meaning of life for myself, I have reopened my mind to the possibility that there is a knowable, universal, independently existing meaning of life that I could someday discover or learn. In the meantime, I don't plan on changing my life path or my goals, but I do plan on being open to change if I feel like I am going in the wrong direction: I don't want to realize at my death that my life was pointless. Maybe I won't realize what I really want in life until five years before I die, but if I am brave enough to live those last five years differently, then at least those five years of my life won't be wasted. Meanwhile, I plan on calling my parents more often, just in case.

AN UNCERTAIN QUEST
FOR CERTAINTY

Becky Grossman

SITTING WITH ME IN Collins Dining Hall for breakfast this week, a friend jokes about the lack of an art department at our school, thankful that she's surrounded by such pragmatic and focused students. We laugh, and I think of how different these four years would be if I had followed my older brother to Oberlin College, that famous Midwestern haven for liberals and musicians. My thoughts wandered to early in the year, when I was filled with frustration and unease in my new environment, doubting my choices, my head reeling with "what ifs."

This second-guessing of my college choice has taken a backseat to recent stresses of schoolwork and friends, but I still sometimes ponder my decision to attend CMC with a hint of regret and self-deprecation, more for the uncertainty than for the choice itself. Uncertainty torments me in many things in life, from daily trivialities

166

to philosophical convictions, and what scares me is that I don't know if the undying quest for knowledge is a fate acceptable to me. Upon first hearing the Lessing quote in class about humbly accepting *the drive for truth* and not truth in its pure form, I pictured myself in that situation, relieved to find an end to the quest and gratefully taking the hand with truth.

It's difficult for me to conceive a quest for truth without a genuine expectation of finding it. The possibility of never reaching that for which I long prompts me to an attitude of cynical defeatism. This would be fine, I suppose, if I could accept a lack of ambition and fall comfortably into a life of blissful ignorance, but for some reason that fails to satisfy me. In trying to puzzle this out, I find nothing unique about myself, but conclude that it is innately human to long for the unreachable truth—and yet few people, obviously including me, fully embrace the inevitable failure of such an endeavor.

Perhaps this is just a maturity issue, and eventually I'll come to appreciate the search for its own sake. It does seem a bit childlike to want stability and certainty in your life, but I suspect that we all, at times, would happily reassume the comforts of childhood. I would wholeheartedly and willingly cling to my childhood nostalgia if that would result in simplicity and contentment in my life. Still, even in that thought I face uncertainty, but is that because there is actually more that I desire or just because society tells me that I *should* want more? No one asks if we want to learn—it's just assumed that we do. Similarly, few expound upon the benefits of knowledge once acquired, and yet society pushes both knowledge and the pursuit of knowledge as unquestionably important.

I think this plays very well—in a somewhat particular sense—into the main thesis of Freud's *Civilization and Its Discontents* (*Das Unbehagen in der Kultur*). Given the social pressure to which I have always been subject with regard to education, I can never quite trust my own motives in its pursuit. Is my drive for knowledge and truth then merely an aspect of conformance, a push toward something in which I really have no interest? Indeed, is this tentative exploration of my *discomfort* (my *Unbehagen*) with this drive simply an aspect of rebellion?

I do not mean to say that society's promotion of something is an automatic reason to reject it. Societal constructs and norms can help to encourage behaviors that are beneficial to the group as a whole in individuals who otherwise might not be inclined to contribute. Consider, for example, a new and completely legitimate idea held only by a minority of visionaries. A community-wide search for truth will force such an idea into wider view insofar as its original proponents feel compelled to disseminate it and the rest seek to understand and to evaluate it. Ultimately then, each new truth brings a deeper meaning into each person's life and into the life of the community. Yet, to take Freud's point more seriously, could it be that society is actually doing harm to individuals for whom truth and knowledge are of no great priority? Are their energies being diverted from goals perhaps less noble-sounding but of more personal meaning? This might be a matter worthy of somber consideration if I didn't think that pursuing truth was deeper than societal structures. I have come to believe that it is a fundamental part of being human and struggling towards what is right.

This leaves me with the feeling that my rejection of the search for knowledge and truth *does* come from a desire to rebel, but not as a matter of indifference to Platonic ideals. Quite to the contrary, I worry that if society is encouraging the quest for truth, it may also encourage certain truths as well, and I don't want to fall victim to truths that are not mine. The possibility of getting it wrong, of discovering truths that are somehow favored by society but inauthentic to me, causes me to back away and to fault the entire process. Still, I realize that I cannot escape the irony that discovering these barriers to desiring truth is in itself a form of finding truth.

While it may be a convenient excuse to say that I'm uninterested in studying for a class because society has pushed a priority upon me with which I do not agree, this does not explain the centuries of thought and discovery that occurred without the pressure of deadlines or grades. It is, however, perfectly reasonable for me to fault those external pressures for my negative connotations with learning. In particular, society's quantification of something that should be without numerical parameters and measurements may well evoke disdain and rejection, and I suspect that this disdain is displaced from the educational system, where it properly belongs, onto what that system is intended to facilitate: the search for truth.

The false absolutes that society values also make me uneasy with the pursuit of truth. Society wants us to find answers, and although, for instance, science calls them theories, they are accepted as truth and become the basis from which other thoughts are born. Society frequently doesn't recognize or acknowledge, as Descartes did, that all things perceived are theories. If society were to advertise this and to drill it into the psyches of its members, it would almost certainly diminish the productivity and the ordinary assurance we take in everyday life. Instead, society functions as if it knows how things are, while the individual must struggle with uncertainty. For me, it becomes personal; it seems as if society has all the answers, and yet, for some reason, I am unable to grasp truth in its pure form. But society's mocking tone rings untrue: society does not have any pure form of truth, and even were it so, I would still want to enjoy the pursuit of truth; it would be a minor barrier to "the knowledge of the abyss."

I could wrap up and dispense with all of the misgivings I've raised here with a nice "but knowledge is worth the struggle" cliché, but my cynicism overrides my poeticism, and I cannot do that. I can, however, concede that I will struggle for knowledge inevitably and will probably remain uncomfortable throughout much of that process. This very discomfort will drive me, however, pushing me to find a place where if not happy, I can at least be complacent. One nice thing about indecisiveness is that truth and goodness can be seen from various angles, and thus I'll never lack for potential truths.

THE LEFT HAND OF GOD

Nina Drucker

ONE OF THE VERY first questions that we considered during our morning session of *Questions of Civilization* was this: "Are you a materialist?" I had never heard that term before, but I soon found that it described my beliefs exactly. Professor Valenza made a distinction between the materialists and non-materialists by asking the following question: If one could obtain the specific duplicate atoms that make up the matter of person X's body and configure them to exactly resemble the physical structure of X (including the atoms in his/her brain assembled with the exact same patterns of wiring and firing and whatever other physical ways experiences are marked in the brain), would the "new" X have the exact same personality, feelings, memories and experiences as the original X? The materialist says, *yes*. In this sense, the materialist does not believe in what most people consider to be a "soul."

The philosophy of materialism is completely rational to me. It is consistent with my well-considered judgments about life and death (which were discussed in a previous essay). Examples taken from daily life may also be used to support this reasoning: When a person hits his or her head and suffers severe brain damage, the personality sometimes changes. Instances of accidents such as this seem to be conclusive evidence for the materialist's belief. Yet even though the view of the world as purely material is thus logical, it leaves me feeling helpless. If my emotions and feelings are simply constructs of physical patterns and chemicals interacting in my brain, then they somehow seem less credible than my "soul's" embodiment of personality and emotional connection to the world. The discussion of the mind-body problem thus leads to questions about how people ascribe meaning to their lives, and I feel prompted to analyze my beliefs.

It may be hard to imagine, but I frequently feel odd about what I believe. There are my intuitive feelings to ignore reasoning, and then there is my reasoning to ignore those intuitions. Can one side win? Do those feelings even matter? My conviction that my feelings are worth something to me is also a construct of my personality that is mapped out on my brain. Someone could open up my skull, give my brain a couple of sharp jabs with her index finger, and 'poof!' there goes my personality! Hence, a paradox is uncovered: initial reactions and gut feelings are a result of different chemicals moving around and other brain activity. By recognizing this, my reasoning tells me that I should be able to step outside of those emotions and rationalize them. If I overreact in a situation, I should be able to recognize my reaction and to attribute it to the chemicals and set pathways in my brain. This analytic process should enable me to halt the reaction and to control my feelings. However, by knowing that my emotions and feelings are superficial, new emotions and feelings arise, and thus the very process I want to short-circuit changes. So I return to the beginning: analyzing my chemical reactions. From this infinite regress, it follows that I will never truly be able to escape those natural responses—no matter how canned they are.

Ultimately, being a materialist should be accompanied by an indifference to death, but for the reasons stated above, it is impossible to rein in my emotional responses. Careful thought leads me to the decision that I would rather be a deep-feeling person, regardless of the origin of those emotions, than force myself through reasoning to complete numbness. Or maybe while reflecting, it came about that I am more inclined to embrace my feelings rather than try to control them—and I have disguised this as reasoning. This gets very complicated because if I never take any credit for the control of my thoughts and feelings, then how can I claim that I have control over my reasoning? The point is that at this moment in my life I recognize that feelings make my life worth living.

About three months ago I became a volunteer for Care Alternatives Hospice in Ontario, California. Hospice is an organization that helps people who are dying to die in peace, without pain, and in their homes (or at least not in the hospital). I am a companionship volunteer. Companionship volunteers exist simply to make the last stages of life as enjoyable as possible for Hospice patients. Patients frequently get lonely and have feelings of helplessness or depression. Families have difficulty stopping what they are doing (working, taking care of the kids, etc.) to spend all day with their grandparent who is dying of cancer. Family members may also become depressed and emotionally unable to cope with such interactions. Companionship volunteers come to be a part of the patient's life and foster a strong connection with a neutral human being. Even if the volunteer simply holds a patient's hand quietly once a week, she can make a considerable impact in those last days and boost the quality of life. Patient-volunteer relationships are frequently very important to the patients.

In order to become a companion, I went through two days of training, got tested for tuberculosis, passed a background check, and was judged fit to volunteer by the volunteer coordinator. To my surprise, a good portion of the volunteer training was devoted to the volunteers' feelings about death, dying, and bereavement. We did exercises such as filling out our five wishes, writing a fake obituary, and deciding what we want done with our body when we die. All these things presumably have not been considered by many people who are not close to death. As is predictable, I went through these exercises in a detached manner, unfazed by my own mortality. I knew it was most important for companionship volunteers to be sensitive to their patients' feelings about death and dying, and I felt very capable of doing that. Had I known the extent of my sensitivity or even empathy, I might have thought a little more about my readiness before taking on Mary, my first patient (whose name I have changed in accordance with my confidentiality agreement).

For the past couple of months I have made weekly visits to Mary. I situated myself in the antique velvet chair next to her new recliner in which she rested, and we just talked and enjoyed each other's company. Although we didn't have much in common, and communication for her became somewhat difficult as the weeks went by, she was alone most of every day and appreciated my visits. Last week I got a call from the Care Alternatives chaplain. She told me not to go visit Mary on Friday because she had just died. I knew that Mary was going to die—that is why she started Hospice care—but I was still stunned. My emotional response overpowered my rationality, and I broke down. I felt uncomfortable and upset, but there is beauty in those feelings.

No matter how conflicting it may be intellectually, I live for the emotional connections and relationships that I make in my life. It is more valuable to connect to other human beings and to take part in the collective experience of being in this world than getting caught up in the race to discover some dispassionate explanation of these lives we live. Living with mystery can be more rewarding than finding the solution, especially because that solution—if it exists—may not be satisfying.

His right hand may tease me, but the left one intrigues me.

THE STRUGGLE TO BE SOMEBODY

Carey Tan

IN LIGHT OF FRANNY Glass's famous declaration in J. D. Salinger's *Franny and Zooey*, I ask myself, "Do I have the courage to be a nobody?" It seems to be a daunting question that would require much consideration before any sort of answer could be found, but in fact the whole question is just false and deceptive. There is no such thing as a "nobody." Every single person born into this world makes some sort of an impact, however small or insignificant it may be. Even if an individual does absolutely nothing else in life, a human being's birth alone changes the lives of his or her parents in some way. Therefore, I do not have to worry about being a literal nobody, because it does not exist. The real question is then, "Do I have the courage to be unremarkable?" and that is a question of substance.

I will confess that I do not at all like the idea of being mediocre. If there is one thing that should be obvious about me, it is that I tend to relish life's extremes, from the highs of passionate, true love to the sorrowful depths of human suffering. I veer away from the middle-of-the-road example of Odysseus and head instead toward the Achilles way of life. There is no doubt that I lack the courage to be unremarkable. Indeed, my fear of being average is one of the biggest motivating factors to achieve success in my life. I have spent the majority of the past twenty years working to be considered above-average, and to this very day I continue to try to push and pull my way up into those higher echelons of achievement. I do not think I am alone in feeling and acting this way; I suspect that most other people are also driven to succeed by an intense desire to be specially recognized for something in their lifetimes. We all want our successes to be noticed and validated by sources outside of ourselves, and we live our lives in pursuit of this validation because it makes us feel purposeful. But this relentless pursuit of something other than mediocrity can be maddening, especially when one stops to consider just what the purpose of it all is. Even I admit, and freely, that living would be a lot easier if I could be content with mediocrity. Without the goal of achieving something extraordinary, I would be free from its stressful demands, which would be a great relief! I see plenty of real-life examples of people who seem to be happy being average. When I'm struggling to write a brilliant paper, such an easy life seems highly appealing. So how can I bring myself to be content with mediocrity?

The *Bhagavad-Gita*, of course, has a lot to say about this subject. Its main teaching is that we should "be intent on action, not on the fruits of action." According to Krishna, we achieve perfect inner peace when we completely detach ourselves from any concerns about the outcomes of our actions. Mastering this discipline would mean that I would be unconcerned about whether my actions would bring me any success. The way of life that is truly unconcerned with the fruits of action would be peacefully complacent, much like the life of non-contention that is described in the *Tao Te Ching*. With such an outlook on life, I would not have to fear failure because I would be just as content if all my efforts amounted to nothing as I would be if they brought me great success and recognition. But the truth is that nothing, not even the *Bhagavad-Gita*, could get us to fully renounce the fruits of our actions and give up extraordinary success. It is an unattainable ideal.

Even the most disciplined, spiritual-minded people are motivated by the fruits of their actions. The Belgian nuns whose motto is "do good and disappear" are no exception. At first glance it would seem as if these nuns have mastered the life of disciplined action that is praised in the *Bhagavad-Gita*. They do good deeds without seeming to want to gain anything from it, as Krishna suggests that we do. But if you think about it, these nuns are really performing these deeds because they believe that God wants them to, and they want to please God. Essentially, these nuns are motivated by the same basic desires as I am. We are all motivated by our attachments to the fruit of our actions, the fruit being special recognition from someone. The only difference here is this: *I look to earn that recognition from other people, while the nuns work to earn it from God.* Thus the nuns only seem to act with the *Bhagavad-Gita*'s discipline.

I should like now to take a deeper look at this point—one that admittedly brings me to a profoundly cynical position. The life of detached indifference to the fruits of our actions may seem desirable for its imperturbable placidity, but, as we have just seen, this it is not as simple as it sounds. Hypothetically, if I could somehow master the discipline outlined in the *Bhagavad-Gita* and truly "be impartial to failure and success," what would motivate me to act at all? What would prevent my contentment and complacency from translating into total non-action? Here the *Gita* greatly contradicts itself. Krishna encourages us still to act, promising that "performing actions for [Krishna's] sake, you will achieve success." But there is a two-fold problem with this statement. First, according to Krishna's other teachings, we are not supposed to perform actions for anyone's sake! He has taught us that we should not act out of *any* desires. Is the desire to serve and please him somehow excluded from that rule? Second, we are also supposed to be completely indifferent to the idea of "success." Yet in his very next sentence, Krishna repeats his demand that we "reject all fruit of action." Does that not mean that we should also reject the success that derives from acting for Krishna's sake? Once I read through all of his conflicting teachings—and here I expose my cynicism—I got the feeling that Krishna only *pretends* to want us to act with complete indifference, but what he is really telling us to do is to act for his sake and not for our own. Thus he urges his followers to live in pursuit of the special favor that he bestows upon those who act on his behalf. Even he realizes that nobody acts without the motivation of gaining the validation of success that we need in order to feel special and important. And since that motivation must always be present in *my* life, I could never truly be content without special recognition for my successes. Even the *Bhagavad-Gita* could not provide an effective argument to prove otherwise.

In the end, a plausible answer to the question of "How can I be content with a mediocre life?" continues to evade me. I do not know if such contentment is even possible, let alone how I may achieve it for myself. For the time being, until I can find a real and undisputable answer, I will assume that no one could truly be content with mediocrity and that it is not even really a desirable way of life. Thus, I shall continue along in my struggle to achieve something extraordinary. And I shall read *Franny and Zooey* this summer....

AS MYSELF AS HUMAN

Cassi Wright

> *The master said: "In words the purpose*
> *is simply to get one's point across."*
> —The Analects of Confucius

WHO AM I? I am an individual, a human being, with thoughts, information, questions, and feelings all whirling throughout my mind. I am open. I am accepting. And I am eager to learn about myself. The self is one of the most complicated pieces of art that I shall ever come across. I am more intricate, complex, and unusual than any other contact I have experienced. My body, my mind, my attitudes, my spirit—all of that makes me *me*. This is me, the all, the everything.

As a person, I have the objective to determine and to understand what I believe. I am young, and even at my age, I have found that this is in no way an easy process. I never dreamt that things that I thought would be so easy would be so difficult. For example, I never thought it would be hard to understand myself. Boy, was I wrong! How do you know who you are if you don't know what you believe? I've surprised myself in more ways than one. As I attempt to discover and to articulate what I believe, I find that the qualities I most admire about myself often cause me the greatest confusion.

My family, teachers and friends have instilled in me that I am not to judge what I do not know. Who am I to scorn something that I have never experienced? If I've never been there, how do I know the rage, pleasure, fear, or love? This has become one of the personal reminders by which I live: *imagining is not the same as experiencing*. I have absolutely no right to judge. From this, I am constantly reminded that I must be open to everything and everyone. I am free to agree or disagree, but I must always take others' views into consideration. Don't ever forget that two people can look at the exact same thing and see something totally different. Part of growing to become the person that I aim to be is to have this degree of openness, especially in admitting shifts of perspective.

I have begun to work this aspect into my daily life, and yet, I am surprised at the ways it has worked against me. In discussions that I've had with other students, we have debated very delicate and controversial subjects, such as homosexuality. I have made the effort to include the other perspectives whether I agree with them or not, and I have found that some people get very defensive and even angry when I raise other views. It's amazing to me that I have received animosity for projecting views that were not even necessarily my own. In this search for myself and the subsequent establishment of a firm sense of boundaries and beliefs, I find that being open seems to cause more and more difficulty.

We read books in class about certain authors' beliefs on subjects, and I take into account all that they say. I find that I understand and agree with contradicting views. Through this class I have found that I am guilty of "walking the fence" on many different issues. And I have found something else: that it's okay. And not only is it okay, it is part of being human.

To be unsure, to question and to be confused is to be human. Otherwise, without these qualities, you might call me God. Everything that I feel is part of being human. Everything that everyone else feels is also part of being human. Isn't it wonderful that no matter what we all go through, it's all right? Whatever anyone goes through, it is part of the process, and the human process consists of so many different events, issues, attributes and emotions that everything is acceptable. How can we ask for more? What could be more satisfying than being part of a species that allows for and includes absolutely everything? I feel so content with knowing that I can feel to any degree and any range, and that it's all part of being in the world. This deep acceptance of the plasticity of being human allows us to accept who we are, all that we feel, and whatever we experience. In this light, humanness itself allows us to feel appreciated. And, as someone once said, "The most desired emotion is to feel appreciated."

Now that I have begun to understand that everything that I feel is acceptable, I feel more comfortable in declaring what I believe because even if certain of my beliefs happen to be inconsistent, it's okay. I have no pressure to finalize my beliefs at this point in my life. Not only am I still in the process of learning who I am, but also of learning who I want to be. When I dream about who and what I want to become, I find a deep affinity with the eastern philosophies. This may be due to the influence from my mother who deeply believes in the peace of the soul and mind and includes meditation as a daily activity. When I read texts such as *Tao Te Ching*, *The Grand Inquisitor* or *The Analects*, I want to pull little phrases from the book and have them imprinted on my mind, so that they are always close at hand.

"Knowing others is intelligent. Knowing yourself is enlightened. Conquering others takes force. Conquering yourself is true strength." Lao-Tzu's words from the *Tao* explain all that I've said and all that I dream. The ultimate experience is to be one with yourself, to know and understand yourself, to accept yourself, and to feel at peace with yourself. I am submerged in this process, and every step from here on out will be a step in the right direction. The final goal of all existence is very personal, but at the same time unselfish. I am to learn to understand myself, but this does not detract from my experience of others; rather it helps me grow in my relationships and to benefit from others as humans. And in heartfelt reciprocity, I want others to be able to benefit from me in just the same way.

Surprisingly, I find complications in the apparently simple business of benefiting from others. The problem arises for me when I am unable to know if I have truly benefited or whether I am simply playing into society's expectations and thereby compromising my authenticity. In my paper about Tolstoy's book *What is Art?*, I said that I was unable to explain my own definition of art because I wasn't able to get past the definition that society has forced me to learn. When I look back on that paper, I realize that I was not simply talking about art, but my life in general. From the minute that I was born, I have grown up in a society that has molded me in a certain way. This is very difficult for me insofar as I am often unable to know if it's the real me, or the me that society has made. In fact, sometimes I wonder if there is really such a thing as the real me.

When I don't act the way that society expects, is that the real me trying to escape? Is it the real me trying to emerge from underneath the weight of the set standard? In *King Lear*, Cordelia declares what she truly feels instead of what society expects. In the *Bhagavad-Gita*, contrary to Lord Krishna's demands, Arjuna repeats that he has no desire to fight and kill the people who are his kinsmen. In *Antigone*, Antigone goes against the state law in an act of sacred and familiar obligation to bury her brother. In these stories, the people who reject society's expectations and begin to let their true selves emerge are banished, persecuted or called cowards. It seems to me that social expectations are not expectations at all, but requirements that I must seriously consider as I explore careers, decide with whom I want to spend my life, and otherwise plan my future. Whenever I attempt to figure out who I am, society flings its expectations back in my face.

Lately, I have begun to feel more and more like J. D. Salinger's Franny: "I'm sick of not having the courage to be an absolute nobody. I'm sick

of myself and everybody else that wants to make some kind of a splash."
(*Franny and Zooey*) This quote is ironic because just two days previous to
hearing it, I had written in my diary, "...I just wonder if my satisfaction is
learned through society. I wish I knew and could decipher the difference
between myself and the being that society made me, but then I guess that's
impossible. Why do I have the feeling that life is not going to get any easier
to understand any time soon? And when I think of my future career, I
know that I don't want to be a doctor or lawyer or something like that, but
I know that I want to be recognized and envied. Why is that so important
to me? Why can't I be happy being 'the nothing, the nobody' if I'm happy
with myself? But no, I want to be the producer or director that everyone
sees and knows about and envies. Why is that so important to me? How do
I learn how to be comfortable with the things that society does not deem
important but that I know make me content with a peaceful soul?"

This direct conflict in my daily life is sometimes almost intolerable.
On the one hand, I am a subject of society's expectations, and I embrace
its materialism. On the other hand, I long for the characteristics that I
read about in the books on eastern philosophy. I long for the fulfillment
that men such as Siddhartha possess. I want to be at the point where I can
say, as in the *Tao Te Ching*, "No self interest? Self is fulfilled." Yet I live in
a completely different world than Siddhartha and Lao-tzu. I must learn
that there are things I cannot change, and therefore I must learn to compromise. Compromising can be one of the most difficult things to accept,
especially when you are compromising with yourself. A major act of compromising for me has been accepting that all my confusion and "walking
the fence" will not necessarily be answered when and where I want. Just
like society, I have expectations that are not always plausible. Realizing this
is the first step in the right direction, and accepting it is a fundamental act
of personal growth.

All my confusion, questions, dreams, and goals are all part of me. And
it is all these things that make me the person who I am. I am no better

than the next person, and no one is better than I. As Kant said, there is no price put on people; we all have dignity and are therefore incomparable. Everyone lives differently, and no one way is best. There are not explanations for everything, and part of being human is not knowing everything that you might want to know. To be human is to be yourself, and to be able to accept yourself for your flaws, for your incomplete knowledge of the world, for the insufficiencies of your own ways.

I need not always question and lament. I quote the *Tao* one last time:

> Knowing that enough is enough
>   Is always
> Enough.

THE POWER OF WORLDVIEWS

Charlie Sprague

A WORLDVIEW IS A personalized intellectual paradigm. One's worldview includes the standards, assumptions, and perspectives that shape an individual's cognitive framework. In this essay, I will address the following question: how do our personal worldviews shape cognition? In doing so, I want to understand how my worldview impacts my thinking, and learn how this relationship between worldviews and thinking impacts our civilization.

The question of how worldviews influence thinking is of great importance to me as an individual and to society. Human beings make judgments and decisions based on a subjective thought process. My own thinking cannot be separated from my worldview, and, furthermore, every member of our civilization has a unique worldview. When judges sentence criminals, politicians decide public policy, and educators teach students, the subjective nature of each individual's mental framework influences those actions. We must accept that the human mind is incapable of perfect objectivity and recognize the influence of mental paradigms on thinking. After considering this question throughout the semester, I have come to two main conclusions about how worldviews shape thinking. First, they cause us to develop different standards of truth and hence govern how we evaluate the world. Second, a worldview not only determines how we interpret the world, but what we are capable of seeing.

It was the differing ontological and epistemological stances of Plato and Aristotle that first drew my attention to the importance of worldviews. In Plato's *Republic*, he develops his theory of forms. The forms are the immutable ideals that we only perceive as faint and distorted copies in our world. Plato argues that, like the prisoners stuck in his famous cave, the world of sense experience deceives people. He says we must transcend these shadows to appreciate true knowledge, knowledge of the forms. Aristotle's empiricism directly contradicts Plato's transcendentalism. In Aristotle's *Nicomachean Ethics*, he examines the world and draws knowledge from experience to understand the components of a virtuous man.

The radical metaphysical split between Plato and Aristotle demonstrates how the search for truth takes place within the confines of one's worldview. In light of the strong teacher-student relationship between Plato and Aristotle, their distinct criteria about what constitutes truth indicates that individuals inevitably develop their own mental frameworks to evaluate the world. The differing conceptions of these two towering philosophers on the source of knowledge caused them to think in completely dissimilar ways. Plato used his reason to transcend the deception of the perceivable world; Aristotle examined the natural world in detail to explain it. Plato and Aristotle's conflicting epistemological standards taught me the importance of worldviews in shaping the standards of truth we use to acquire knowledge. Donald Davidson's quotation "Every sentence is a theory" perfectly captures my sentiments. Whenever we make assertions about the world, those statements reflect our standards of truth that stem from our own worldviews.

Thomas Kuhn's *The Structure of Scientific Revolutions* further stimulated my interest in the effects of worldviews on thinking. Kuhn's argument that paradigm shifts define scientific revolutions exposed me to the subjectivity inherent even in scientific pursuits. What struck me most was Kuhn's argument that when paradigms shift, scientists do not simply reinterpret the data, they actually observe different objects and forces. The passage that introduces Chapter X summarizes this idea: "[T]he historian of science may be tempted to exclaim that when paradigms change, the world itself changes with them. Led by a new paradigm...scientists see new and different things when looking with familiar instruments in places they have looked before." According to Kuhn, Platonists and Aristotelians may have had distinct observations when they studied the world of Ancient Greece. Due to the powerful influence of paradigms, Kuhn argues that geocentric astronomers and Copernican astronomers did not simply have contradictory interpretations of data, they actually saw space differently. When I read about how scientific paradigms affect observation, I realized the same principle must apply to individual worldviews. The logical extension of paradigms influencing community observations is that individual mental frameworks must shape what people perceive.

The ability of a worldview to impact one's sense of reality finds its best expression in the conflicting epistemic stances of the sisters Eleanor and Marianne in Jane Austen's *Sense and Sensibility*. As we discussed in class, Eleanor observes the world, objectifies it in light of community standards, and then verifies her beliefs; Marianne, too, begins with her senses, but goes on to conflate reality with her own narration. Thus Marianne's mindset encourages her to see and feel true love in Willoughby's actions because Marianne's imagination colors her perception. In contrast, Eleanor's worldview causes her to sense much less sincerity and passion in Willoughby. The contrast between Eleanor and Marianne reveals how their unique paradigms lead them to experience the world entirely differently.

Kuhn's idea that worldviews influence perception connects with my previous knowledge on related topics. In the psychology courses I have taken, the power of top-down processing has always fascinated me. In one shocking experiment to demonstrate the principle of intentional blindness, a large percentage of people fail to notice a man walking by in a gorilla suit during a basketball practice, when, naturally, the audience expects to see only basketball training. In the study of linguistics, George Lakoff's *Don't Think of an Elephant* examines the political implications of cognitive structures. He notes that when people study politics, they pay attention to certain pieces of information and completely ignore other pieces based on previously established mental frames. Whether watching movies, reading political advertisements, or conducting science, individual mental frameworks dramatically influence sense perception.

My conversations about God with our classmate Blake this semester have exemplified the importance of worldview in shaping one's thinking. In every aspect of his life, Blake senses, feels, and knows God's existence. God is an essential *property* of Blake's thinking. In contrast, my picture of the world includes no supernatural beings; my worldview is inseparably tied to my atheism. Our distinct personal paradigms accordingly influence our perceptions of the world and our epistemological standards. For example, walking back from class one day, Blake and I exchanged ideas on the beauty of nature. Blake talked about how he sees and hears spirituality in the natural world. But when I find myself in beautiful locations, I have no conception of this spirituality. Instead, I see a completely different type of beauty, one that amounts to appreciating the wonderful power of natural selection, geological patterns, and the exceptional qualities of earth as a planet.

Blake and I do not even try to convince each other of the correctness of our perceptions and positions because our standards of truth depend on our worldview. Like the scientists arguing from separate paradigms in Kuhn's book, he and I are individuals with irreconcilable worldviews. Any attempt at conversion would fail because our arguments for or against the existence of God depend on a kind of circularity: ultimately our beliefs are logically embedded in axioms that cannot be logically or empirically resolved. Along these lines, after reading Richard Dawkins' entertaining and informative book *The God Delusion* this year, I intend to read Leo

Strobel's *The Case for a Creator* with an open mind out of fairness to this important metaphysical question. I am doubtful it will have any impact on me, however, because of the circularity problem. Thus the fundamentally different worldviews of the atheists and believers prevent rational or scientific arguments from changing either side's position. Paradoxically, recognizing this, while clarifying the nature of the argument, diminishes the value of debating the existence of God.

The interaction between my worldview and my thought processes will continue to affect my life. I am a student committed to a process of intellectual growth at an institution of higher education. The many components of my worldview—atheism, liberalism, and numerous other features—color this learning because my studies take place within my own mental framework. The beauty of my collegiate education, however, is that my college years offer me the opportunity to expand and enrich my personal paradigm. During my freshman year, I have challenged my assumptions, been influenced by respected professors and peers, and sensed noticeable changes in my worldview. Worldviews will also impact my future career as a professor. When I teach college students at a later date, I must be cognizant of the reality that my students will not share my personal paradigm. I will try to make my lectures, discussions, and assignments accessible to students of diverse intellectual frameworks. I trust that my constant awareness of my subjective mindset will help me with the struggle against bias when teaching.

My semester in *Questions of Civilization* has exposed me to how individual worldviews dramatically influence thinking. My previous knowledge, exposure to Plato, Aristotle, Kuhn, and Austen, and my conversations with Blake all affected my opinion on this important issue. Let me reiterate at this point that I believe worldviews have two critical impacts on cognition: they determine how we evaluate the world by causing us to establish standards for truth, knowledge, and belief, and they affect our experience of the world by in part determining our perceptions of the world. Consequently, the importance of worldviews in shaping thinking necessitates constant awareness. As an individual, I must carefully guard against the danger of mistaking my personal worldview for an objective assessment. As a society, we must strive to promote tolerance and an acceptance of ideological diversity because the temptation always exists for the powerful to impose their worldview on others.

LIFE AS PERFORMANCE ART

Ashley Baugh

LIFE IS THE ULTIMATE form of performance art. Every day we are adding a brushstroke, a new color, a new shape to the portrait of our lives. Each action, inaction, thought, hope and comment brings more definition to what will be the final product. Those whom we bring into our lives can change our pallet of colors from bright yellows and oranges to deep blues or browns, depending on how they affect us. Our life paths add shapes, forms and content to the scene. Every day each of us makes decisions about what will be in the final piece: what will be hidden in the background, what will be in the foreground for all to see, and what impact it will have on those who have born witness to it. The greatest responsibility we have to ourselves is to incessantly reevaluate what we are striving to leave on this planet after we depart, and then to decide if we like the art we are creating. However, often we get caught up in the day-to-day processes of life.

Thus far, I feel that my art has developed well; there are elements of disappointment, accomplishment, happiness, heartbreak, pride, and love. I am trying to bring in as many bright, happy tones and shades as possible without denying that you cannot see real life while wearing rose-tinted glasses. I also want to give more depth and glow to my yellows and oranges by contrasting them with the darker shades of life. Life is not always perfect, but it is the imperfections that create the flawlessly blissful moments. Art and artists that only convey one-dimensional happiness create a false image that is ignorant of the pain and suffering within the world; this pain does not cancel out the happiness, but, quite to the contrary, gives it more depth by providing a stark contrast. It is thus my belief that the end result of a life canvas more richly textured with times of strife and suffering, as well as with stretches of contentment and joy, is able to convey more meaning. This is to say that I will be more able to communicate my life's message when not all of my experiences have been positive.

The image *Felicity Wishes XVI* by Emma Thomson is an example of what I do *not* want my life to be like artistically. It lacks any sort of meaning because it exists only to be unnaturally happy, a caricature of real life. While it is happy, it is superficially so. It represents the happiness of a child who has yet to realize that life is not perpetually idyllic; it is not that I hate this optimism, but I would rather gather real experience even at the expense of all my happily-ever-afters.

A life that is too picture-perfect often lacks profundity, and is unable to communicate any significance. Those who

Felicity Wishes: Spectacular Skies, Emma Thomson,
Reproduced by permission of Hodder and Stoughton Limited

have not had to struggle do not question the foundations of their life paths as seriously as those who have encountered strife. I hope that by the time I complete my life, I have struggled to create *and* to appreciate my accomplishments.

This is not to say that the only enlightened life is one of perpetual struggle. Like anyone, I want my final work to be filled with happiness; I want to attract and to keep people in my life that make me happy, and I hope to reciprocate by adding joy to their lives as well. Those who become wrapped up in sorrow and misery as the only form of truth are just as foolish as those who refuse to see pain and suffering. The world is filled with beauty in both physical elements and actions. As we learned in *You Shall Know Them*, humans are a very distinctive breed; we have an active conscience that continues to produce heroic and selfless deeds that have to be more than just an evolutionary reflex. Both the characters Antigone and Lear's daughter Cordelia acted in selfless ways out of a strong sense of morals and love that would not be seen in the animal kingdom. If we cannot recognize beauty such as this within ourselves, within others, and in the world around us, we are doing a great disservice to the human species and our own lives.

L'Absinthe by Edgar Degas, 1876

If, upon our deathbeds, we have created a work of art that only focuses on sorrow and tragedy, we have created a very disappointing and inaccurate portrait. I feel strong pity for anyone who feels that such an image is a true portrait of their lives. An example of such a work is *L' Absinthe* by Degas. The characters are detached from one another and cold; the sorrow is beyond words and simply looking at it makes the viewer so sad that she must look away. The colors are dull blues and grays; there is no excitement or happiness to be found. Degas is one of my favorite artists, and this is one of the most memorable paintings that I have ever seen, but this is the last painting I would ever choose to create with my life. I do not want to be an emotional black hole that drains all those who come into contact with me of any happiness.

What I want is somewhere between these two. I want the depth that comes from enduring challenges, but the ability of a child to hope. I want to create something beautiful, but realistic. I want to look back at the art of my life and say that I had a good balance of happy and sad tones and themes.

It is not important that my life be a masterpiece; I do not need to be famous or recognized by all. In fact, I would prefer to have a piece that is hated by some, and loved by others. I am not interested in being a generic or iconic piece of work that everyone loves. My biggest desire is that my life have balance: balance between bright and dark colors, joyous and sad themes. I do not want to create art just to please others, but I do hope that others enjoy what I create; I hope that I can draw people to my life that *I* enjoy and who enrich my life.

My life portrait is only eighteen years in the making, and I hope that I am still far from completion of the project. But the closest artistic representation of what I hope my life will be is the *Stoclet Frieze: Expectation, Tree of Life, Fulfillment* by Gustav Klimt (middle section shown below). It portrays love and anger, joy and jealousy, colors that are both bright and dull. There are swirls that are both beautiful and confusing but add to the general aesthetic appeal of the piece. There is a richness in detail that seems like there is nothing left unsaid—and that is how I want to leave my life, having done everything and covering every inch of canvas.

While this is the closest work of art to what I want my life to be like, it is not the perfect piece. I, like everyone, am unsure of how my final work will turn out. The hardest thing to remember is always to reevaluate what we are creating and to ask ourselves what we are putting into the world. Are we producing something that others will want to walk away from, upset at even seeing it, or a work that will make them stop—if only for a moment—to drink in the beauty we have created. It is so easy to forget the final picture, and to get caught up trying to make the day-to-day work. Ivan Ilych is an ideal example of someone who was too busy pursuing false leads of happiness to keep in mind what he wanted his life to look like at the end. One must continually reevaluate his or her creation, and what is frightening is that we can never be sure that what we are creating now is what we will want on our deathbeds. By continually questioning and reevaluating who I am, what makes me happy and what I want from life, I am trying to create a final portrait of my life that is as close to what I want it to be as possible. Socrates said, "The unexamined life is not worth living." I am trying my best to examine myself and my life as much as possible in the hopes of creating a work of art of which I will be proud.

Klimt Tree of Life, MAK-Austrian Museum of Applied Arts/Contemporary Art
Photograph: © Gerald Zugmann/MAK. Reprinted with permission.

An Ivory Soap Lesson

Courtney Dern

I WAS AN 8ᵀᴴ-GRADE girl. And, like many 8th-grade girls, I was on top of the world; the queen of my middle school domain. I had friends, lots of them. I had a boyfriend who gave me bears on Valentine's Day and *the* silver-stripped Adidas shoes. I had it all. And, to top it off, I had a week-long trip with my class to San Diego for Sea Camp.

One part of our trip involved spending a day at Sea World. I was very eager for the day to arrive. When it finally did, my land-locked-Colorado-born-and-raised self grabbed the thick black sunglasses that I had been sporting at the time, put on a brightly colored spaghetti-strap tank top, laced up those Adidas shoes (the ones that matched those of nearly every girl on the trip) and headed for Shamu.

We were allowed a great deal of freedom within the park. So, armed with disposable cameras, metal mouths, and high hopes, we made our way through the sea of activity, carelessly navigating the multitude of sun-screened bodies. We traveled together to the various attractions offered—enjoying being under the California sun instead of our parents' watchful eyes—in an army of ego, a flirtatious gaggle. The girls cooed at the sea-otters. The boys coveted the sharks. Everything was light-hearted and predictable.

Then, in a rare moment alone, I wandered off from the group. We were in the Arctic exhibit, so I made my way through the cool, dim underground hallways. I remember glancing absentmindedly at the informational plaques covering the fake stone walls. I think there was a soundtrack playing aquatic animal noises. This pathway led me to an underground tank, one where you can see the mammals swimming below the surface of the water. It was the beluga whale exhibit.

And there they were: the two most beautiful creatures I had ever seen. If you have ever seen one, you know that the beluga's serenity will tighten your throat. I stood there, breathless, with the blue light of the water projecting onto my skin. I swear they were carved out of soap: flawless, ivory soap. I instantly fell in love with those perfect marble statues gliding through the water.

It felt like I couldn't open my eyes wide enough. I wanted to see them on a larger scale than physically allowable. The disposable camera was out of the question; nothing could capture their glory. Words could never do them justice. So I just stood there, enveloped by their beauty and humbled by their presence.

What a perfect world they must live in, I thought. I was mesmerized with the simplicity of their lives. Surely they must be happy; they are living in an Arctic Olympos, without a care or threat in the world. But then came the obvious recognition of their barred, unnatural condition. So I amended my thoughts accordingly: it might be nice to be a wild beluga, cruising nature's icy oceans up at the crown of the globe.

Then, seeing my own manifestation in the glass, I realized how unnatural I felt. Looking at myself in the foreground of the giant mammals, I thought about how easy it was to live conventionally. Of course those were not my words back then, but God, I felt shallow. My Adidas, my popular shirt, all of my outside appearance had been created by convention. I was weakened by my own triviality. I realized that I'm really good at playing the convention game; it is easy for me to fit in.

But, in my disparity, there shown a twinkling in my eye, a reflection of the white monsters swimming peacefully across my pupil. It took two tons of majesty, but I noticed them. I mean, I *really noticed them*. And, at the same time, I really noticed me. I was so aware of our authentic existence that my eyes swelled and I was able to internalize their power.

When I was finally able to blink, I looked around at the families surrounding me: a dad in a baseball cap, sharing an ice cream sandwich with his son. I remember the son's little arms and sticky face. I remember the dad's graying hair and loving eyes. There was also an old woman sitting on a bench, clearly enjoying the relief from the heat. She had on a matching red outfit. I thought of her deciding to wear that outfit that day; it warmed my heart. There we were, illuminated in the soft blue beams from the tank, perfectly human. It reminded me of how everyone looks beautiful in campfire light. None of it was trivial. I was humbled and amazed at all that I noticed. Those creatures taught me something truly precious that day.

I thank the beluga whales for my tremendous appetite for awareness; I constantly try to notice more. I want to notice that aspen trees look great in snow. I also want to notice *the choices that I choose to make*—and there is no redundancy in this phrase. Neither do I want to be religious because it is how I was raised, nor do I want to wear Adidas shoes simply because everyone else is. And I do not, with every cell of my creation, want to be an Ivan Ilych.

We really take notice when we are not afraid to face the subtleties that color the world, or the major themes that we live by. Now, more than ever, I understand the value of asking myself the most difficult questions. Because I value the search for authenticity, I cherish the self-inquiries. These are the questions that we will never be able to answer. They are also the questions that are exceedingly important to ask. In order to make sure that I am still singing my own song, I will continue to ask myself these questions of civilization that help me to define who I am and to interpret the society in which I live. It would be almost effortless to see my reflection purely as a successful product of a popular teenage girl. At that moment, however, looking at those belugas, I was completely aware that I was more than that. I am more than a byproduct of societal norms, and I am more than the molecules that compose my organs. It is easy to lose sight of something so simple. Sometimes it takes two tons of beluga to make you notice who you are.

The most personally significant moments of my life have arrived through this utter awareness of self, situation, and other. Perhaps it is this metacognition that helps make us human. This drive toward consciousness has helped influence my place in the world. I want to study psychology and anthropology. I want to understand the components of our minds that in part compel us to think and act the way we do. I want to notice the cultural themes so innate that we fail to see them at all. To me, the study of people is the most relevant topic in the world. For the same reason, I am also attracted to literature. The emotional connection words provide allows for the expression of countless human qualities. At the same time, however, I love the fact that some things are entirely inexpressible.

When I think about the different forms of relationships and beauty that exist in the world, I feel like I can't ever open my eyes wide enough. I'm pleasantly straining to see it all. When we understand our drives and emotions, we are able to choose our actions with deliberation. Since we are not caged in a zoo and since we possess freewill, this awareness makes all the difference.

So, sing in me, whales. Sing in me because I, unlike you, am not bound by Plexiglas. In an exquisite paradox, I returned to Plato's dark cave when I emerged from my Arctic depths. Down in that cavern I experienced beauty and truth, and because I am blessed with a sense of agency, I am able to return to the light of the real world in order to share what I learned. In order to get anywhere, it is vital that we work together in this universal quest for truth. Sing in me because I am able to share a sense of perfect humanness—a borderless sense of self and others—and still possess an internal and private individuality. Sing in me because I am human.

References

INCLUDED HERE ARE BIBLIOGRAPHIC entries for the most commonly cited texts in this collection.

Aristophanes. *Clouds* in *Four Texts on Socrates* (translated and with notes by Thomas G. West and Grace Starry West). Ithaca: Cornell University Press, 1998.

Austen, Jane. *Sense and Sensibility*. New York: Penguin Books, 1995.

The Bhagavad-Gita (translated by Barbara Stoler Miller). New York: Bantam Books, 1986.

Confucius. *The Analects* (translated by Raymond Dawson). New York: Oxford University Press, 1993.

Freud, Sigmund. *Civilization and Its Discontents*, the Standard Edition (translated and edited by James Strachey). New York: W. W. Norton, 1961.

Greene, Graham. *The Quiet American*. New York: Penguin Books, 1996.

Homer. *The Odyssey* (translated by Robert Fitzgerald). New York: Vintage Classics, 1990.

Lao-Tzu. *Tao Te Ching* (translated by S. Addiss and S. Lombardo). Cambridge: Hackett, 1993.

Morrison, Toni. *Beloved*. New York: Vintage Books, 2004.

Plato. *The Republic* (translated by G. M. A. Grube, revised by C. D. C. Reeve). Cambridge: Hackett, 1992.

Plato. *Apology* in *Four Texts on Socrates* (translated and with notes by Thomas G. West and Grace Starry West). Ithaca: Cornell University Press, 1998.

Salinger, J. D. *The Catcher in the Rye*. New York: Bantam Books, 1964.

Salinger, J. D. *Franny and Zooey*. New York: Bantam Books, 1964.

Sophocles. *Antigone* in *Sophocles I,* Second Edition (translated and with an introduction by David Greene). Chicago: Chicago University Press, 1991.

Tolstoy, Leo. *The Death of Ivan Ilych* in *The Raid and Other Stories* (translated by Louise and Aylmer Maude). Oxford: Oxford University Press, 1982.